The Disadvantaged Early Adolescent:
More Effective Teaching

McGRAW-HILL SERIES IN EDUCATION
HAROLD BENJAMIN, Consulting Editor-in-Chief

ARNO A. BELLACK *Teachers College, Columbia University*
Consulting Editor, Supervision Curriculum and
Methods in Education

HAROLD BENJAMIN *Emeritus Professor of Education*
George Peabody College for Teachers
Consulting Editor, Foundations in Education

WALTER F. JOHNSON *Michigan State University*
Consulting Editor, Guidance, Counseling, and
Student Personnel in Education

SUPERVISION CURRICULUM AND METHODS IN EDUCATION
ARNO A. BELLACK *Consulting Editor*

BATCHELDER, McGLASSON, AND SCHORLING •
  Student Teaching in Secondary Schools

BENT AND KRONENBERG • Principles of Secondary Education

BROWN, LEWIS, AND HARCLEROAD • A-V Instruction:
Materials and Methods

BUTLER AND WREN • The Teaching of Secondary Mathematics

LEFEVRE • Linguistics and the Teaching of Reading

MARKS, PURDY, AND KINNEY • Teaching Elementary School
Mathematics for Understanding

MASSIALAS AND COX • Inquiry in Social Studies

MICHAELIS, GROSSMAN, AND SCOTT • New Designs for the
Elementary School
Curriculum

PHENIX • Realms of Meaning

STOREN • The Disadvantaged Early Adolescent:
More Effective Teaching

STRANG, McCULLOUGH, AND TRAXLER • The Improvement
of Reading

WINGO AND SCHORLING • Elementary School Student Teaching

The Disadvantaged Early Adolescent:
More Effective Teaching

Helen F. Storen

Professor of Education
Queens College of The City University of New York

McGraw-Hill Book Company

New York, St. Louis, San Francisco
Toronto, London, Sydney

The Disadvantaged Early Adolescent:
More Effective Teaching

Library of Congress Catalog Card Number 68-13528

1234567890VBVB7543210698

The Disadvantaged Early Adolescent:
More Effective Teaching

Library of Congress Catalog Card Number 68-13528

1234567890VBVB7543210698

The Disadvantaged Early Adolescent:
More Effective Teaching

Helen F. Storen

Professor of Education
Queens College of The City University of New York

McGraw-Hill Book Company

New York, St. Louis, San Francisco
Toronto, London, Sydney

The Disadvantaged Early Adolescent:
More Effective Teaching

Helen F. Storen

Professor of Education
Queens College of The City University of New York

McGraw-Hill Book Company

New York, St. Louis, San Francisco
Toronto, London, Sydney

The Disadvantaged Early Adolescent:
More Effective Teaching

Library of Congress Catalog Card Number 68-13528

1234567890VBVB7543210698

To: Jeanette, Natalie, and Kenny

PREFACE

For a number of years it has been my privilege to work closely with preservice and beginning junior high school teachers in the slum areas of large cities. Anyone with similar experience is aware of the fact that many young teachers become discouraged and transfer as quickly as possible to middle-class neighborhoods or to the more affluent suburbs. Others stay on and cynically settle for "keeping order" or routine teaching. Those who accept the challenge struggle through a difficult first year and achieve the joy and satisfaction that can come from helping disadvantaged youngsters learn to learn.

Teachers in the junior high schools invariably have a more trying time than the teachers in the elementary schools. Part of the difficulty is due to the pattern of organization of the junior high school. Although certain features of this "in-between" school have proved superior to the traditional elementary school, the fact that the slum child who most urgently needs close associations and consistent guidance is thrown into a labyrinthian plant and scheduled to meet six or more teachers each day, who are in turn responsible to three or four administrators, mitigates against his getting the kind of sustained individual attention he needs. The instructor may teach from four to six different classes—sometimes on different grade levels—making a class register of approximately one hundred. To try to do the sort of individualized teaching that is recommended in the college method classes is almost impossible.

A few junior high schools are now changing organizational patterns and are arranging "little schools within a school" so that the teacher will have fewer pupil contacts, and pupils will need to make fewer adjustments to new teachers during the three-year period. If the trend continues, the task of the junior high school teacher should be somewhat less harrowing.

Another reason why junior high school teachers find their assignments frustrating is that in most school systems there is little vertical curriculum planning. The seventh-grade curriculum plans frequently fail to take into consideration the achievement level of the disadvantaged children who are accepted from the elementary school. Add to this the lack of appropriate teaching materials and often inadequate supervision, and it is no wonder that the teacher mortality rate in junior high schools is so high.

A plethora of books and articles has been written in the past five years about the slum schools. Sociologists have developed graphic descriptions of the slum areas, and psychologists have tried to explain why a larger proportion of poor children, chiefly Negroes in most of our large cities, are academically two to three years behind the overall population. Bad housing, poor nutrition, segregation, and discrimination, as well as poor schooling, have taken their toll; and it may take at least another generation to see appreciable change. The crash programs in the early grades such as Project Head Start may ease the situation, but it will be some time before these children reach the junior high. Nor will greater integration, the way it is proceeding, solve tomorrow's problems. Wherever the disadvantaged child takes his seat, he will need compensatory education.

The city schools are not so bad as they are painted by some of our popular writers, but neither are they as good as they should be if our disadvantaged youths are to be able to compete with their more fortunate peers. These schools need not only *enough* teachers, but the best teachers.

Everyone would like to wave a magic wand and bring all children up to grade level by next September. Consequently, with the best of intentions, all sorts of schemes and devices are being explored. Extravagant claims are made for new curricula, team teaching, programmed books and other materials, extended school days, and special guidance facilities.

Projects abound, but seminal research into the learning process and the teaching act is just beginning after a hiatus of years when educators neglected the cognitive aspects of learning. Until the bits and pieces of research are put together and implications for actual classroom practice are set down, we shall have to "make do" with what we now know and what we can learn from the teachers in the field.

Teachers colleges always take the brunt of criticism for any failures of the schools. In this case, I believe we should accept our share of the blame—at least for not recognizing soon enough the need for a concentrated effort to analyze the needs of teachers in the inner-city junior high schools.   We are now painfully aware of our weaknesses and are frantically modifying our programs.   Education students are given large doses of sociology and anthropology, and the foundations of education courses include strong emphasis on the problems of inner-city schools.   Yet, knowing about the slums and the families who live there will not make a good teacher.   As important as this information is for a teacher's general background and as sympathetic and understanding toward the slum children as the college student may be, this is no guarantee that he will be able to cope successfully with a classroom of reluctant learners.

It is in the methods classes and in student teaching that the future teachers must learn the skills necessary to teach these students.   They must learn not only the principles of teaching and learning but the way that these principles apply to the actual classroom situation, which is, for most college students, unlike the schools that they attended.

During the past few years, the methods classes at our college have used considerable material which we collected from teachers in the field. Because this material has appealed to students and has served as a good basis for class discussion, we wish to share it with other college instructors. All the incidents, quotations from teachers' diaries, and children's comments included in this book are real.   Some of them were collected over a period of years from my own observations and from in-service teachers in my courses. The greater part of the information comes from the Bridge Project,[1] a study carried on by the Queens College department of education from 1960 to 1965. During that period, we worked with three young teachers, all Queens graduates, who taught three classes of disadvantaged children from seventh through ninth grade.   These teachers, who taught the four academic areas—English, social studies, science, and mathematics— recorded their experiences weekly. We believe that their self-evaluations together with the exchange of ideas with the project coordinator and college staff enabled them to solve many prob-

[1] The research reported herein was supported by the Cooperative Research Program of the Office of Education, U.S. Department of Health, Education, and Welfare.   Additional support was provided by the Board of Education of the City of New York and the Board of Higher Education of the City of New York, New York Foundation, New York Fund for Children, Taconic Foundation, Nathan Hofheimer Foundation, New York Times Foundation. The Public Education Association acted as sponsor.

lems encountered by all beginning teachers in slum schools./ It was with the encouragement of the Bridge Project Committee that I decided to select material from the reports as a basis for this book.   Much of the interpretative material and the comments, however, are my own, and I should not want to hold my colleagues responsible for my particular enthusiasms or biases.

Chapter 1 gives a very brief summary of the characteristics of disadvantaged youth.   Chapter 2 takes up the problem of discipline because this is the greatest area of concern to the young teachers getting ready to teach in the inner city.   Chapter 3 focuses on diagnosing the students' needs and readiness.   The heart of the book is contained in Chapters 4 and 5, which deal with content and method.   In these chapters most of the teacher-related incidents come from the Bridge Project. / A few of the incidents, particularly those at the end of the chapters, are taken from the recordings of another group of beginning teachers who were prepared at Hunter College.   This material was part of the TRUE Project [2] with which I was associated for one year.[3]

After each chapter there are a few questions for discussion or an incident or problem to analyze. The instructor and student will, of course, think of many other questions to clarify or challenge the content in the chapters.   A selective reading list is also included and should be supplemented with the latest periodicals.

This book differs from other books now available on disadvantaged children because (1) it treats the junior high school years which have not heretofore been studied as carefully as the early elementary years; (2) it contains records of teachers analyzing their own problems, experimenting with various ways of working and achieving some measure of success; and (3) it is addressed directly to future teachers who seem to respond well to this kind of approach.

It is hoped that classes using this book along with their regular methods texts will be able to project themselves into the situations

---

[2] *Teachers and Resources for Urban Education,* Hunter College of the City University of New York.   (A grant from the Office of Juvenile Delinquency and Youth Development, No. 62201.)

[3] Most of the teachers' comments quoted throughout the book are taken from tape recordings.   They have not been edited and consequently may not always meet the criteria of written English set for teachers.   It seemed to us that editing, or asking the teachers to do so, would take away from the spontaneous and emotional responses the teachers gave when they related their experiences.

described and to analyze and challenge the ideas presented. It will, we hope, help them to see that the job will not be easy but that it can be rewarding.

In-service teachers may also find the book interesting if only to compare it with their own experiences.

Helen F. Storen

ACKNOWLEDGMENTS

My first acknowledgment must be to the memory of Dr. Leonard Kornberg, who had the foresight and vision to initiate the Bridge Project, and who, with the assistance of Mrs. Richard Loengard of the New York Public Education Association, obtained the funds some time before "deprived children" became a popular cause. To the other members of the Bridge College Committee, Dr. Robert W. Edgar, director, and Dr. Albert J. Harris, and to the coordinator, Dr. Gertrude Downing, I give my thanks for not only permitting but encouraging me to select from our joint report appropriate material for this book. Many of the incidents, particularly those related in Chapters 4 and 5, have appeared in a short pamphlet prepared for our methods classes by Dr. Robert W. Edgar and me and made available in mimeograph form by our college.[1]

I wish to express my appreciation especially to the teachers, Miss Jeanette Doerler, Mrs. Natalie Mintz, and Mr. Kenneth Tewel, who laboriously recorded their experiences over the entire three-year period and who built, with the coordinator, a truly professional and democratic situation which enabled them to find in teaching difficult children a deep intellectual experience as well as a satisfying emotional one. My thanks go, too, to Mr. Robert Lovinger, the psychologist of the project.

My gratitude must also be expressed to the members of the Board of Education of the City of New York, the administration of the junior high school where the project was carried out, and to all my colleagues and students who participated.

A second source of live material comes from the TRUE Project at Hunter College. Here I have used material taken from recordings of teachers during their first semester of teaching. I wish to thank

---

[1] This booklet bears the title "Learning to Teach in Difficult Schools." It contains incidents and questions for discussion.

Dr. Marjorie Smiley, director of this project, who was most helpful in my efforts to organize this material for use in college classes.[2]

For typing at various stages of preparation my appreciation is given to Miss Jane Brown and Mr. Norman Bailey.

[2] Helen F. Storen, *The First Semester,* TRUE Project, Hunter College of The City University of New York, 1965.

CONTENTS

The Disadvantaged Early Adolescent:
More Effective Teaching

Chapter One
What Can I Expect?

Imeet classes five periods each day. Some days I have the same class for two periods. One class has twenty children and the others between twenty-five and thirty. All are Negroes and most of them from very low economic backgrounds. One class is considered an average class and two are below average —one is the second lowest on grade. The classification is supposedly homogeneous, but it is really only roughly so. In one class, the reading range goes from about four to seven. Most of the lowest group are virtually non-readers. However, I know already that some read much better than their scores indicate. Even in the lowest group some read faster and understand better than others.

I have been given one set of literature books, one seventh and one fifth grade level—but nothing that the slow group can read. I am supposed to teach remedial reading to one group but I do not have any material and I have had no preparation for this. So I shall probably just concentrate on reading comprehension.

They are a very unpredictable class. You don't know what they are going to do next. They are easily offended, they get very angry very quickly and they have no control over their feelings. If you don't call on them, they become real angry or they will crumble their paper and put it down. Their behavior patterns are really so childish. It is almost as if we were dealing with a group of third or fourth graders.

The social studies syllabus is totally unsuited to these students. Three-quarters of the work that students are expected to cover has no meaning to them. I refuse to inflict any more material on them for which they have little use and which serves only to frustrate them as well as to damage further their self-concept. Such pupils come to an educational dead end in a school like this, and it should be considered one of our primary objectives to find a suitable program for them to follow.

Do you think the above descriptions are typical of the conditions faced by beginning teachers in slum junior high schools?

Who are these children and what hope is there for making up their deficits?

Why and how are they different from middle-class children?

The best judge of the specific abilities, attitudes, and aspirations of a class is a good teacher.   You will make your own judgments when you begin teaching.   The following brief discussion will simply give you an overall picture of the kind of students you may teach if you work in a poor economic section of a large city.

Many hasty statements based upon inadequate data or meager experience were spread over the pages of periodicals a few years ago when the cause of the poor first became popular.   Since then, educators and journalists have become a little more cautious in expressing opinions and making generalizations, but you will still need to check broad assertions and to hold opinions tentatively.   One group of new teachers had been told, or read in an article, that slum children were apathetic.   When they began teaching, they were amazed to find that many students in their classes were not at all apathetic but on the contrary overly anxious about their schoolwork.   The person who had tagged disadvantaged children as apathetic may have been judging from a small sample; or perhaps he did not realize that the same children may be apathetic in one situation and not in another. A major danger of acting hastily on research conclusions is that by the time a study is published, certain basic conditions in the situation may actually have changed.   From our observations over the past six years in one particular underprivileged area (90 percent Negro), we have seen many of the

Negro children become more assertive and more confident. This could be because of the progress of the civil rights movement and the awareness of the more dynamic Negro leadership. With these cautions in mind, we can now look at a few summary statements made by sociologists, psychologists, and educators who have concerned themselves with the education of the disadvantaged.

THE PROBLEM OF LABELS

The terms *culturally deprived, disadvantaged, alienated, slow learner, inner-city child,* and *slum child* are all used imprecisely and interchangeably in the current literature. By the time this book is published, there will be new labels. Rather than trying to justify one term over another, we, too, shall use these labels interchangeably. This seems permissible as long as the reader knows that we are always referring to pupils who have a cluster of characteristics in common. The young people we are talking about in this book have not learned the academic skills at the normal rate. They live in poor city neighborhoods. Most of them are Negro or Puerto Rican. There are, of course, children who are below grade level in middle-class communities but not nearly as many of them as there are in the slums. We need to remember, too, that in these urban slums there are some children who compare favorably with middle-class children in academic and social abilities, but these are the ones who have in some way escaped the usual effects of poverty and discrimination. Because of a century of neglect and discrimination, most Negroes have not been able to move as swiftly into the middle class as white Americans. Although the opportunities are growing each day, a much larger proportion of Negroes than whites are still living marginally, and often even those who do have an adequate income must live in a ghetto because of housing restrictions. Our focus then will be mainly on the large number of children in the city schools who have learning problems and who continue to make poor adjustments to the school program.

ACADEMIC ABILITIES

In our country as a whole, between 15 and 20 percent of the school children do not learn the academic skills at what would be considered the normal rate. In the large urban areas, the percentage is twice that. By the time such children reach the junior high school, they are two to three years behind grade norms in the academic areas. Because of the rigidity of the graded system, the pupils continue each year to be up against a curriculum which is too demanding. These cumulative deficits tend to weaken the ego and frequently cause frustration, antagonism, and even rebellion. It is not surprising that many pupils drop out as soon as they reach the leaving age. And it is no wonder that a young teacher finds her beautifully prepared "motivations" making no impact.

At this point someone is bound to ask, "Do these children really have the potential or is it a waste of effort to try to bring them up to grade?" The children in these slum areas do fall below children in middle-class areas on the tests of mental ability. In typical inner-city schools, although the range of ability may run the gamut, the mean IQ score will range from 85 to 90, which is well below the mean in most middle-class communities. The current belief about intelligence is that although it has some innate base, its realizations and directions are determined by experience and that it should be viewed as something which grows and develops.[1] It is believed that the difference is due to the deprived environment of the slum child. Recent studies of intelligence indicate that stimulation and structure are necessary for normal intellectual development. Studies also show that not only lack of intellectual stimulation but lack of strong emotional relationships may affect a person's mental development.

The obvious answer to these deficiencies is, of course, to try to provide the necessary experiences at an early age.

[1] For an excellent summary of intellectual development of deprived children, see A. E. Tansley and R. Gulliford, *The Education of Slow Learning Children,* Routledge and Kegan Paul, Ltd., London, 1961, chap. 2.

Project Head Start and other enrichment programs are now widespread. However, it will be several years before the children involved in these programs reach the seventh grade, and if the elementary school does not continue to provide more and more challenging experiences, the children may slip back.

Research provides data which show that children placed in a better environment frequently have raised their test scores ten points or more.[2] Even adult IQ scores have been known to be raised by more favorable circumstances. The important thing for the teacher is to understand what the disabilities are that show up on the tests and to try to give students learning experience in these areas. Frequently the lowest scores that disadvantaged students receive are on vocabulary and information—areas the school can definitely help to improve. Other shortcomings, as evidenced by test scores and observations by teachers, are (1) poor speech habits, (2) short attention span, (3) difficulty in building concepts and making generalizations, and (4) difficulty in dealing with abstractions and in classifying and problem solving. All these disabilities can be checked by informal measures if the teacher doubts the validity of the tests.

Poverty and discrimination have left their toll, and the schools, to date, have not adequately compensated. There are children of all races and all places who are deficient in cognitive skills, and there are multiple causes for this condition—both physical and environmental—some of which, at the present time, no teacher can remedy. However, there is enough evidence now to indicate that there is hope for reducing the deficiencies which exist in a disproportionate number of children of the urban poor.

PERSONALITY CHARACTERISTICS

The second quotation at the beginning of the chapter describes a seventh-grade class which acted like babies. An-

[2] Benjamin Bloom, Allison Davis, and Robert Hess, *Compensatory Education for Cultural Deprivation*, Holt, Rinehart and Winston, Inc., New York, 1965, p. 12.

other teacher in a different school makes a similar observation.

One of the reasons why this group is so difficult is because of the large number of problem cases in that class. Almost every child in the class has a physical, emotional or mental (low I.Q.) problem. I am only one person. I cannot help every child at the same time. Over and over I find myself saying, "Just a moment, I have to finish with John," or "Save your individual problems until the whole class gets settled." Each person expects an immediate response to his query, if not sooner. He CANNOT wait. He has no inner controls. This is a world of babies in the bodies of teenagers when it comes to waiting, or exercising controls. The only way to handle a group of children like this effectively is to keep it small.

The immaturity noted by these beginning teachers is characteristic of many disadvantaged early adolescents as evidenced by personality-test results and observed by therapists and guidance counselors.

The results of the Rosenzweig picture-frustration test, given to 147 children in the Bridge Project school, are relevant here.[3] Compared with the normative group, the present population is markedly and significantly more extrapunitive and less intropunitive. This means that when they are frustrated, they are more likely to hit out in an aggressive fashion than to blame themselves or try to explain the situation away. The most striking conclusion from the results of this test is that the total pattern of this group more nearly approximates the normative pattern for the eight-year-olds than it does the normative group of twelve- or thirteen-year-olds. The immaturity is, of course, far more marked in some members of the group than others, but for the group as a whole, it stands out as a significant finding. Results of the Rorschach Ink

[3] See Gertrude Downing, Robert W. Edgar, Albert J. Harris, Leonard Kornberg, and Helen F. Storen, *The Preparation of Teachers for Schools in Culturally Deprived Neighborhoods* (The Bridge Project: Cooperative Research Project no. 935), Queens College of The City University of New York, Flushing, N.Y., 1965, pp. 141–142.

Blot Test with the same group also show that these children were somewhat less mature than the normative group.

It is interesting to find that these same conclusions are reached by studies of English children in poor circumstances. Tansley [4] reports on the immaturity of retarded children in the schools for the educationally subnormal, stating that some of them continue to seek affection very much as pre-school children do. They also react to frustration with temper tantrums and childish sulks. He concludes that this may well be because of inadequate satisfaction of basic needs when they have been deprived of play, recognition in the home, and attention.

When both parents work, there is not always time to explain to an adolescent why he should behave maturely. He may simply be told, "Do this." Overresponsibility in having to care for young children and to take on household chores may also make these youths desperately *want* someone to pay attention to them, and the only way they can get this attention is to misbehave and act like babies themselves.

Disadvantaged children also tend to lack strong egos. "The available evidence does seem to indicate that ego development of the deprived child is more likely to be characterized by lack of self-confidence and a negative self-image than that of the middle class child. This is particularly true for the Negro deprived child who suffers the additional handicap of a caste-like status and prejudice." [5]

You may expect then to find many of the young adolescents you will teach responding in a childish fashion. They may be immature emotionally as well as mentally. On the positive side, personality tests reveal that these children often have a keen awareness of social situations. The students in the Bridge Project showed up to be somewhat more socially responsive and more sensitive to finer shadings in social situa-

---

[4] Tansley et al., *op. cit.*, p. 50. (The English children designated as educationally subnormal are a rough classification of backward students whose IQ range is from 60 to 90. In many ways they resemble our children in this same IQ range.)
[5] Bloom et al., *op. cit.*, p. 72.

tions than the middle-class groups with which they have been compared.[6] This is understandable when we think about the crowded living conditions that slum children encounter daily and their constant contact with personalities of all ages. The lack of involvement with hobbies, with reading, and with national or current events puts a premium on close human relations and imposes a burden heavy to bear.   On the other hand, these relations develop a sensitivity in the slum child, which the middle-class child, who can escape by himself or go off during a family fight, does not have.

CONCLUSION

If you decide to teach in a large city, you will very likely be assigned to a junior high school where the students are socially and academically handicapped.   They will come from homes where the intellectual, aesthetic, and cultural advantages are meager.   Although there may be care and affection in the home, poor economic conditions may make it impossible for many parents to provide the warmth that is needed.   In more of these homes than in middle-class homes, the father is absent or the children are living with surrogate parents.   The schools and community have not provided the compensatory experiences needed particularly for the Negro child, who bears the scars of two hundred years of alienation.   Better housing, more jobs, and more social opportunities should eventually make a difference. Meantime each teacher in the slums faces the challenge of doing his part in this movement for delayed justice.

The content of the remaining chapters is taken chiefly from the experiences of young teachers, showing the day-to-day problems they faced, how they reacted to them, and in some cases how they achieved a measure of success.   As you project yourself into the situation, try to think deeply about why they failed and why they succeeded.

[6] Downing et al., *op. cit.*, p. 151.

QUESTIONS FOR DISCUSSION

Read at least one of the references listed under "Suggested Reading" and prepare to discuss the following questions.

1. Why do you think that the concern for the disadvantaged has increased in the past ten years?
2. Who is responsible for the failure of such a large proportion of these children to achieve at the normal rate?
3. What are some of the areas of disagreement among educators concerning:
   a. Significance of intelligence tests
   b. Specific academic deficiencies of these children
   c. Personality characteristics of these children
4. What types of compensatory education programs seem to the experts to give promise? In what areas is further research needed?

SUGGESTED READING

Bloom, Benjamin, Allison Davis, and Robert Hess:
  Compensatory Education for Cultural Deprivation,
  Holt, Rinehart and Winston, Inc., New York, 1965.
Crow, Lester D., Walter I. Murray, and Hugh H. Smythe:
  Educating the Culturally Disadvantaged Child,
  David McKay Company, Inc., New York, 1966, chaps. 1–3.
The Educationally Retarded and Disadvantaged,
  The Sixty-sixth Yearbook of the National Society for the Study of Education, edited by Paul A. Witty,
  The University of Chicago Press, Chicago, 1967, chaps. 1–3, 5.
Frost, Joe L., and Glenn Hawkes:
  The Disadvantaged Child,
  Houghton Mifflin Company, Boston, 1966, chaps. 1–3.
Gordon, Edmund W., and Doxey A. Wilkerson:
  Compensating Education for the Disadvantaged: Programs and Practices: Pre-school through College,
  College Entrance Examination Board, New York, 1966, chaps. 1, 2, 7.
Strom, Robert D.:
  Teaching in the Slum School,

Charles E. Merrill Books, Inc., Columbus, Ohio, 1965, chaps. 1, 2, 7.

——— (ed.):
The Inner-city Classroom: Teacher Behaviors,
Charles E. Merrill Books, Inc., Columbus, Ohio, 1966, pp. 21–41.

Tansley, A. E., and R. Gulliford:
The Education of Slow Learning Children,
Routledge & Kegan Paul, Ltd., London, 1961, chap. 2.

Chapter Two
Establishing Rapport

In Chapter 1 we described the characteristics of young adolescents in our inner-city schools. Such information, although essential as background, does not seem to make much impact on the middle-class college student of education until he actually begins to teach. Most new teachers experience a shock when they get into the classroom. Their chief problem is almost always their inability to "control" a class, and they frequently complain that their college education courses have not prepared them adequately. The following comments, listed by teachers in the slum schools of a large city, are typical:

I cannot control the class.

The children are excitable; throw things; are restless.

There are three or four seriously disturbed children in each class.

They all talk at once.

I found the class getting completely out of hand.

Utter chaos broke loose.

They want constant attention.

They chatter ceaselessly and make a tremendous amount of noise.

General disorder and inattention seem to be the regular behavior pattern in a large proportion of the new teachers' classes.

In addition to complaints about the classes as a whole, these beginning teachers describe the behavior of individual children:

Elizabeth will sit quietly in class, sucking her thumb, leaning down on the desk and then all of a sudden in the middle of a period she'll let out a blood curdling yell and start cackling, and then I'll look at her a second and she'll stick her thumb back in her mouth and go back and lie down on the desk again.

One of the boys drives me crazy. He always folds his eyelids back and it drives the other kids crazy. They think it's very funny.

John went over to Currie and started fighting—sort of wrestling and I couldn't tell how serious it was until Currie took the pointer from the front of the room and cracked it over John's head. By the way, he broke my good pointer.

There are a number of discipline problems in the class. Today one of the girls had an outburst, completely unfounded. Something must be bothering her at home. I don't know. I asked her for her homework and she reacted violently and told me she wasn't going to do it.

It is easy to see why teachers become discouraged. Pressed with all the tasks of the first few weeks of school, they go home heavily ladened with guilt and a sense of failure. None of the gentle admonitions, the carefully prepared lessons, or even threats of punishment seem to result in an orderly classroom where students can learn. A few of the pupils, like some of these described above, may be seriously disturbed—even psychotic. If such behavior is frequent, these children probably need professional guidance or therapy beyond the skill of a classroom teacher. A young teacher should not be dismayed when he cannot turn such deeply disturbed boys and girls into responsive self-controlled individuals. In fact, these students should be removed from the regular classes or placed with a more experienced teacher.   The beginning teacher should make referrals to the guidance office, consult school social workers, or obtain whatever services are available in the school system.   In the meantime he will have to settle for temporary solutions.   Now we shall look at the question of general disorder, which, although it can be more provoking than the misbehavior of one child, is actually more easily controlled.

Overall chaotic conditions may be partially due to poor administration, inappropriate curriculum, or lack of proper materials; but often these class "eruptions" are caused by a teacher's lack of planning and his inability to adjust to children who have developed little self-control and whose response reactions differ from those of children who have been trained to accept corrections in silence.   Their past experiences, both at home and at school, may have taught them to respond only to harsh discipline, and consequently they cannot always understand or trust a more moderate approach. If the teacher lacks inner security and poise, he will be threatened by a pupil's defiance; but if he is a normally mature young person with balance, perspective, and some sense of humor, he will accept the challenge of a disorderly class and eventually learn to cope with it.   Although the majority of beginning teachers have difficulty with at least the *worst* class (and there is always *one* that is given to a new teacher), some of them succeed even with these groups by the time the first term is over.   This can be illustrated by the following college students' observation reports of a school in a neighborhood not unlike the ones described by the teachers at the beginning of the chapter.

Mr. C's lessons are presented in a relaxed manner and the students remain seated while participating in the discussions. When the need arises, Mr. C. will ask the student to speak in a louder voice so that everyone can hear him.   Mr. C's students, who are all slow learners, appear very much involved in the subject matter; in addition they seem to admire and respect him.

At J.H.S. "Y" all the classes I have observed, the teachers seemed to have close relationships with their students and the students seemed to enjoy being in school and working with their teachers.

How did the teachers in this school achieve such a fine atmosphere? Perhaps the analysis of ways of establishing rapport and coping with disorderly pupils that are discussed in this chapter will enable you to think more objectively about your attitudes toward discipline and enable you to avoid some of the pitfalls that await most beginning teachers.

Attention will first be given to the question of motivation, and then we shall turn to such mundane topics as classroom organization and routines and to a few specific do's and don't's for handling common kinds of misbehavior.

It will be well to remember at this point that many discipline problems are caused or intensified by lack of appropriate curriculum and method. The selection and organization of learning experiences will be treated in Chapters 4 and 5. This chapter, which deals *directly* with discipline, has been placed first because it is almost always the first concern of the teacher. He thinks he cannot teach until he gets the children to behave. In reality it may be the other- way around; that is, if he teaches well, students will behave, but these two factors are so interrelated that it is hard to separate them.

MOTIVATION

A beginning teacher, discouraged because he is unable to maintain an orderly classroom, may seek the help of his supervisor, who often responds with the cliché that if students are *motivated* to learn, the discipline problems will disappear. But what *exactly* does motivation mean, and how do you go about achieving it? The young teacher recalls from his college courses that different people mean different things by motivation, and even those who agree upon a definition may differ in their suggestions for classroom practice.

Certain textbooks use the term *motivation* very broadly, others in a very restricted sense. A psychologist may focus his discussion entirely on unconscious motivations, and the young teacher wonders what *he* can do about that. A methods instructor may talk about making subject matter interesting or relating the content to the child's immediate concerns. The teacher maintains he has tried this with little success. Certain textbook authors treat motivation entirely in terms of extrinsic and intrinsic, and many of them frown upon extrinsic motivation as a very low form of stimulation and doubt its effectiveness. Perhaps for our purposes we should not argue too much over definitions but talk mostly in the concrete about how to help disadvantaged pupils *want* to learn.

If students become engaged in learning, they will not disturb others but will respond to direction and guidance, and the teacher's discipline problems will more or less disappear. What are the specific things a teacher can do to get a class concerned about learning?   First of all, it is wise to remember that all students will not respond to the same stimulus. If an adolescent comes to school with a curiosity about rockets, animals, or cowboys, he will sit down and eagerly read a book on the subject, provided it is on his reading level.   If another pupil is starved for affection and attention and a teacher gives it to him, he may do anything the teacher asks him to do.   A third student, because of a sequence of failures and discouragements, may not respond to any topic or any teacher. He has developed a negative attitude toward school, and can no longer see any connection between his needs or goals and what he is supposed to learn.   He will disrupt the class, sit and sulk, or wander aimlessly around the room.

It will take a good bit of knowledge about each pupil and considerable experimentation with different techniques to begin to overcome the negative attitudes of children.   However a few research studies and the experiences of successful teachers do give a few clues to effective motivation.

Tangible Rewards

The selection of appropriate subject matter will be discussed later, but at this point we need only say that this alone will not always keep all children working at all times.   There is considerable agreement that disadvantaged children need more tangible and immediate rewards than children who have developed academic interests or who have accepted long-term goals, such as entrance to college.   Two studies that support this thesis are summarized in Bloom.   Until the disadvantaged child has strengthened his ego and developed a trust in his teachers and their ability to help him so that he is sufficiently motivated to widen his horizon and extend his goals, the teachers need to use any kind of incentive which will help the student to take the first step.   Once he has achieved even a small measure of success, he may take the next step by himself.   For a splendid discussion of extrinsic and intrinsic motivation of the disadvantaged, see Ausubel's article in *School Review.*[2]

Teachers have reported success with all sorts of old-time measures which tended to be discarded during the Progressive era, such as gold stars, trophies, prizes of all kinds, candy, entertainment, trips, banners, placards, displays of children's work, privileges, and classroom jobs of responsibility.   Because of the slum children's emotional immaturity, certain of the prizes that appeal to them would never do for more sophisticated or mature children.   All these rewards, of course, must be used only if the goal is achievable by the child and if individual or class progress is stressed rather than excessive competition.   One teacher reports:

As far as rewards are concerned, Donald who is definitely a discipline problem seems to respond to anything tangible.   He loves the *red checks* I give for doing his homework.   He goes around showing it to the other children.   "See I got it right!"   Other children too insist that the mark be put on their papers in big letters.   I know this is not intrinsic motivation, but it works.   They are settling down and they are actually beginning to learn and want to learn.

Another teacher used another kind of tangible reward to teach an English lesson.   He promised the class that those who wrote very good announcements for a school-sponsored

[1] Benjamin Bloom, et al., *Compensatory Education for Cultural Deprivation,* Holt, Rinehart and Winston, Inc., New York, 1965, pp. 171–172, 178.
[2] David P. Ausubel, "A Teaching Strategy for Culturally Deprived Pupils: Cognitive and Motivational Considerations," *The School Review,* vol. 71, pp. 458–463, Winter, 1963.

movie could read them or have them read over the public-address system. The fact that they were being recognized encouraged them to work hard on an exercise that might have been just another English chore. Students also love to make their own booklets, class newspapers, or posters—anything which will display their wares. With insecure and slow children the teacher must be sure to display even the "not so good" paper if it is the best the child can do at that time.

Praise

Even more effective than the "gold stars" is a well-deserved word of praise.

Upon complimenting one boy on his work I found his face light up and saw how satisfied he was with his work. Others whom I did not compliment were quite upset. They seem to need praise to stimulate them to do better work.

Hurlock's classic and often quoted studies that praise is better than blame but that both are better than indifference seems to be particularly applicable to the disadvantaged. Holbrook says it nicely in describing his experience with English children in the "C" stream.

Whatever the reason, it is true that they need unlimited approval and only endless approval produces results from such children. And the simple act of approval works wonders. The teacher only has to cultivate the habit of saying and writing "Good!" "Excellent!" "Well done!" instead of "Bad, Fair, or Slovenly." Many teachers mark down in the mistaken belief that if children have it "too easy" they will slack. I am not sure about this with brighter children. . . . But with "C" and "D" stream children it does not work at all. They are "marked down" already and have been for years. They are rejected and despised by men. Negative criticism merely reinforces their sense of failure and disables them.[3]

[3] David Holbrook, *English for the Rejected,* Cambridge University Press, London, England, 1964, pp. 207–208. (These "slow learners" resemble disadvantaged American children in many ways. They come from lower-class homes and are often the victims of past failures.)

Motivation should be viewed as a continuous process, and when working with deprived children, you need to use all your ingenuity, insights, and imagination to incite them to learn.   You may never succeed in having a quiet classroom; but if you succeed in developing a desire for learning, this will provide enough order to enable you to teach.

ORDER AND STRUCTURE

Muus in his excellent little booklet *First Aid for Classroom Discipline Problems* points out that deprived children need an organized world rather than an unorganized or unstructured one.[4]   It may be that because of a disorganized (and even sometimes chaotic) homelife, such children consciously or unconsciously crave order in school.   They want to know where they are going, and although they may have a difficult time keeping quiet or getting down to business, they are continually "shushing" each other—telling each other to "shut up" and asking the teacher to get rid of the troublemakers.   As one youngster wrote, "One thing my teacher do he let the children run all over—that is what I don't like about my teacher.   My science teacher I like because he makes us work."

A teacher has to learn how to provide both freedom and order.   This is not an easy task.   You will have to remember that you will probably never have perfect attention from a group but that children cannot learn in an atmosphere of confusion and disorganization.

Children of the slums are often anxious or compulsive or both.   Too much freedom of choice may increase their anxiety.   Teachers should provide positive directions but at the same time indicate that disruptive behavior is unacceptable in the classroom.   The child may then find it possible to develop some internal control.[5]

---

[4] Rolf Muus, *First Aid for Classroom Discipline Problems,* Holt, Rinehart and Winston, Inc., New York, 1962.
[5] See Pauline Sears and Ernest Hilgard, "The Teacher's Role in the Motivation of the Learner," *Theories of Learning and Instruction,* The Sixty-third Yearbook of the National Society for the Study of Education, The University of Chicago Press, 1965, part I, chap. 8.

Daniel Levine's extensive experience leads him to similar conclusions.   He says that the lower-class student responds to regularity of pattern because the student is accustomed to responding only to direct orders and has not been taught self-discipline.[6]

Consequently a classroom should be so organized that there is a minimum of confusion.   In addition to well-organized subject matter, appropriate activities, explicit directions, and adequate time allotment, routines of housekeeping should be established from the beginning of the term.   A teacher tells how important this aspect of teaching is.

I find that one area in which I was inadequately prepared for teaching by the college was the matter of routines.   Only a teacher, having taught in the situation we are in, can really appreciate the importance of knowing how to prepare a class adequately either for a discussion, for moving furniture, for the distribution of papers, for lining up, for taking the attendance, or for collecting materials.   The mechanics of running a classroom is possibly the most important aspect of getting off to a good start in a school like ours.   A teacher can either succeed or fail depending upon the effectiveness of his routines and procedures. . . .   I have changed my attitude toward routines this second year.   I will very often build my lesson around certain routines, such as homework, or exercises at the beginning of the period.   John Dewey might frown at this approach, but I doubt if he ever tried to get Arthur to do any work.   Although the classes may need some of these routines now, they may not be as necessary in the ninth year.

Seating Arrangements

Frequently we hear young teachers say, "You can keep your movable seats.   They create chaos."   They tell of the noise and confusion in moving the chairs, the tendency of the children to push and shove, and numerous other problems created by not having tacked-down desks.   At this point the

[6] Daniel A. Levine, "Differentiating Instruction for Disadvantaged Students," *Educational Forum,* vol. 30, no. 2, pp. 144–145, January, 1966.

teacher seldom sees any advantage to using various seating arrangements.   However, toward the middle of her first year one teacher seems to have discovered for herself the value of movable desks.

I have come to the conclusion that the seating arrangement should depend entirely upon the type of activity that is to be engaged in.   If there is to be committee work, the desks should be turned so that five or six pupils are facing each other in a circle.   If a few children are giving a little dramatization or demonstrating something, the rest of the class should be in a large circle facing them.   If pupils are doing individual written work or working in teams of two, the desks may be arranged in the conventional rows.   I learned the hard way that moving desks is a skill that children have to learn.   Consequently the teacher must spend time teaching the children how to reorganize the desks.   Otherwise there is chaos.   These children need very specific directions for everything.   They always need to know what, why and how; moving chairs and passing out materials are not exceptions.

Responsibility

Providing an orderly classroom and insisting upon ground rules does not necessitate armylike organization—nor require a martinet teacher.   Students need to be given a share in making certain decisions and appraising their own behavior.   Self-discipline comes slowly, but one of the best ways to ensure it is for the teacher to gradually give students responsibility.   When students have specific jobs to do that they think count, they often cease being restless or "lazy."   As they acquire the habit of doing things on their own without being prodded every minute, they often transfer this habit to other chores and routine schoolwork.

The two comments below on what students like about teachers are evidence of the joy of responsibility—to be able to *do* something and to be trusted to do it.

I like them when they let me go on erens and when they let me do something like erase the black board.

I like to work in the office. I put stamp on the mail and weight them. . . . the telephone and working at the switchboard. I enjoy it very much. Their is much excitement. Maybe some-day I will work in and office and get good money.

In one class a child finally came to life and learned to read chiefly because she was given the responsibility of watering plants. Mary was from a broken home, and had been shifted around from aunt to grandparent to foster home. She had failed the previous year and was now repeating the seventh grade with a teacher who took some interest in her. She was a nonreader, restless, sullen, and sometimes violent. She walked around the room constantly and could not settle down. The teacher gave her the responsibility of watering the plants. This required her to leave the room, get the water, and bring it in. It usually took up the first half hour. However, after this productive activity she settled down and was calm for awhile, and eventually the teacher was able to reach her. Armed with a third-grade mystery story, Mary settled down, learned to read, and made great improvement.

Sometimes these children will not do their assigned jobs well—these jobs may take too much concentration or other students may prevent them from doing them. But if the teacher is patient, it is usually possible for the children to succeed, and with success comes the feeling of satisfaction and pride. Again one must remember the emotional level of these adolescents. More mature seventh or eighth graders may resent being asked to do little jobs, such as erasing the blackboards or counting the books, but these pupils will clamor for such jobs. They can also be given responsibility for taking the roll, alphabetizing papers, collecting home-work, and getting material from the library. A few junior high schools now arrange to have the students help with younger children if there are some in the same building or nearby. They may also act as group leaders when going on a trip or developing a project. You need to be prepared to have some failures, but one of the best ways of achieving good rapport is to let the students know that you trust them and to give them another chance when they make mistakes.

CIRCUMSTANCES NOT UNDER YOUR CONTROL

A teacher thinks he has established routines, delegated responsibilities, and planned meaningful experiences, and in comes a class like a "tornado." (This is probably the day the supervisor also drops in.) Sometimes the textbook writers and the school administrators forget that the barometer, the day, the hour, a neighborhood crisis, or a playground incident may "set a class off." Here is one teacher beginning to question her response to the after-lunch problem.

I always seem to have trouble with the sixth period. I notice that when they come back from lunch—they are all worked up and can't be controlled. They all have to go to the bathroom. They all want to run out of the room. They are thirsty—they are exhausted—and they don't want to work. And this is a great disturbance during this period. I've also noticed that I am much too harsh with them. I am very, very strict and stern. And in a way they interpret this as not liking them, so they revolt. I think what I have to do with this class is just stop and begin all over again—right from the beginning. Not as far as the work is concerned, because we have made some progress, but in terms of my attitude toward them and their discipline.

There is no foolproof prescription for dealing with these incidents, but this teacher was trying to think it through in terms of her own attitude and behavior. Perhaps she might let them blow off steam for a few minutes, or maybe she could put on a recording and play some music until they quiet down.

Friday Afternoon

Friday afternoon is another bad time. Like the teacher, most students are eager for the weekend. There has been some speculation that slum children may react in an obstreperous fashion on Friday not because they are eager for the weekend but for a different reason. It may be that they do *not* look forward to the weekend because their homelife may be either lonely or chaotic, and as the time draws near, they act out their fears and frustrations. One distraught teacher thought a change of routine might help on Friday afternoon.

It was during the last period on Friday that I had my least successful lesson. The lesson was to be a spelling pre-test and I felt that something different would be a pleasant change for them so I decided to let some students work at the board. I selected about five students to go up to the board and the rest of the students were to work in their seats. The ones at the board seemed to be more concerned with penmanship and neatness than the actual spelling of the words. Utter chaos came after a few of the words were repeated. They kept saying, "Go slower," and they kept erasing the words and trying to make them look nice. After the first five words I decided that it was enough. I had everyone sit down and I continued dictating the pre-test. After dictating I then asked for individual students, as I normally do, to spell the word to see if it was spelled correctly, and put it on the board so that those who didn't spell it correctly could correct their paper. I feel that this lesson was not successful because it required too much moving around. I learned students shouldn't be encouraged to be so active on Friday afternoon.

Maybe it was not that the students could not take a change, although frequently any shift in routine does incite these children, but that the reasons for the new activity were not explained. (In fact it makes you wonder what the point was in this case.) Directions and timing also should have been more explicit.

Some teachers think it best to have a quiet lesson on Friday afternoon.

I felt good last Friday because my discipline was a lot better. On Friday afternoon the best thing to do is to have a quiet lesson. And I found myself giving the children tasks where they would be working at their seats silently, and I might read a paragraph to them and we would discuss it; or I might do a demonstration—but nothing exciting because they themselves were on edge and all their energy seemed to be just waiting to explode. All this energy that they contained all week long, and I just felt that I should take Friday a little bit easier.

Many of the problems that occur at crucial times are intensified by the teachers' personal reactions.   No two teachers are alike—some are calm, others ebullient; one is witty, another solemn.   Students learn to appreciate the various types as long as they know that the teachers respect them.   Some teachers ride the waves on Friday afternoon and permit a little disorder without being upset and without the whole thing getting out of hand.   Other teachers may feel that they cannot operate with any confusion on Friday and therefore must plan more formal lessons.

Holdovers

Another circumstance that a teacher cannot control is the policy of "holding over" or not passing a child.   The beginning teacher often finds that the three or four troublemakers are students who are repeating the grade or class.   "This class has several holdovers and they resent this.   They refuse to do the work and say it's 'baby-work' or 'we had this.' "   The holdover boys and girls are usually larger than the other pupils, and they often "lord it over" the smaller ones.   They act out their hostility and their fear of continual failure.   If the school will not change this holdover policy, the teacher has to devise some way of helping these students gain self-respect and still inspire or motivate them to work to capacity.   Until he can diagnose their problem (see Chapter 3) he will have to capitalize on their known assets, give them something to do that they can do well, counsel with them individually, and appeal to their sense of pride.   Because they probably can do some things better than others, he may ask them to help the other children instead of replying as one teacher did, "If it is such baby work, why do you fail all the tests?"

Fights

Eruptions of temper sometimes occur even in a well-organized classroom.   Very excitable children may react to a seemingly trivial incident out of all proportion. "There was a fight in class yesterday. L. (boy) hit P. (girl) while my back was turned and P. called him a few four-letter words. I just shoved them apart, one to one side of the room and one to the other and told them to sit down." This male teacher in a no-nonsense manner and few words settled the problem at least for the class period. Women teachers, being afraid to interfere, may well respond less calmly and may simply have to get out of the way and call for help. If aggressive behavior persists, it calls for investigation and guidance; but often these episodes, which could be tolerated on the playground, demand firm and immediate action if they occur in the class-room. More often than not fights take place in the room of an inexperienced teacher where students have not yet learned the degree to which he will put up with such behavior. After rapport has been established and rules are accepted, most youngsters will control their aggression at least until class is over—unless, of course, they are provoked beyond their control.

A FEW THINGS TO REMEMBER

Don't Yell

I like teachers that do not yell in your ear. I dislike nosieie teachers.

I don't like school because all the teachers do is yell at you.

When the teacher tell you something you so post to do and if you don't do what he said he got to hallow out his ear drums to get it thru your head.

It is a sad but true commentary that the amount of shouting and screaming in the slum schools often exceeds the amount of teaching. Although the effect of screaming on a child's ego may not be as bad as physical punishment, it seldom has the desired effect of quieting down a classroom for more than a few minutes. Because for the first few times yelling will bring a child to attention, new teachers continue to use this method, and as time goes on, they hardly realize that they are doing it.   If tape recordings could be made as one walks down the school corridors, the teachers might be shocked to hear their own vulgar screeches.   It would seem almost anything would be better, flashing a light, tapping on the desk, or even blowing a horn!   If a voice must be raised on occasion, perhaps to prevent one child from harming another, this may be excusable, but to scream constantly for attention must indeed be as nerve-racking to the class as some of its behavior is to the teacher.

Learn to Listen

I think some teachers is very unfare.   When they see something wrong they do not try to find out the true.   They won't let you explain.   They pick on whoever they think did the thing and maybe it's the wrong one.   They allways say, "I took you for an example," while the guy is laughing at the one who was picked. This always happens to poor me.

With the intention of trying to get a class back to order a teacher may almost unconsciously blame a child who has a record of misbehaving and refuse to listen to his explanation. This is fatal, and even if it takes awhile, the teacher should let the children explain or tell them he will hear their explanation after school.

A Second Chance

The best teacher I like is Mrs. S. because she gives you first and second chance, but if you is bad the third time she will not tolerate with you.   Some teachers are just to nice and the children take advantage of them.

Most students want a firm teacher and one who maintains an orderly room, but like adults they resent arbitrary, uncompromising actions.   Most good teachers find that students' misbehavior is often spontaneous and that they will acknowledge their faults and appreciate a second chance. If the action is repeated, a positive appropriate punishment, such as staying after school to make up wasted time, repairing the damage, or apologizing will be effective.

On Being Human

New teachers often are told that they must be sure not to "act like a pal," and consequently they assume an aloof, formal, and distant manner. Also they may be so concerned or frustrated by the innumerable chores and clerical jobs that they ignore a child's request or fail to respond to his friendly overtures. One pupil summed up his reaction this way:

The things that I like about teachers is that sometimes they understand you, they give you the mark that you deserve. Some are kind to you and they repeat important things to you. They act like themselves and they treat you like you would like them to treat you. I also think that they should teach in a manner that you would understand.

DIS LIKE! When you see them in the morning and you say, "hi"—they don't answer you they make believe they don't see you. They consider little things like it's a crime. They don't act like themselves. Just because they are older they treat you like babies.

As the teacher gets "his hand in" and gets to know the students, he should be able to "be for real" and still maintain his dignity. Developing a classroom situation where warm friendliness prevails but order is maintained takes time and skill.

CONCLUSION

Young adolescents in inner-city schools have more problems and usually have less inner control than their peers in middle-class neighborhoods. The young teacher cannot be shocked by the misbehavior and will need to work out his own scheme for providing an atmosphere for learning. In the next chapters the focus will be on providing the kind of experiences which should minimize behavior problems. Here it has merely been suggested that the teacher not forget the importance of positive approaches, such as praise, tangible rewards, responsibilities, and routines. There are no absolute prescriptions because good interaction depends to a great extent upon the unique personality of the teacher and the particular needs of each class.

QUESTIONS FOR DISCUSSION

The following account was recorded by a beginning teacher during the second week of the term. Read it carefully and be prepared to give your reactions to the questions listed at the end of the account.

"The Sweater Girl"

This week my official class really got out of control one period and I just about managed to keep my head above water. The class really hasn't settled down as yet. Now, if you can see the picture: stuff piled all over my desk because I had not been able to get at it; roll not taken that noontime; lesson not very well prepared. I was tense and nervous and very anxious to keep the class under control. (I've been told so much about that first day and that first week and how important it is to establish a good image of yourself that I have tried to give all my attention to students' needs and neglected the clerical work.) Well, this particular day a student ambled into class real late, after the second bell had rung. In a couple of minutes she came up to my desk. "I want to go back to get my sweater," she announced. Well, I actually had every intention of allowing her to get her sweater, but for the time being I just wanted to get the class settled so I said, "Sit down, Denise," and she kept saying, "I want to get my sweater," very insistent. I said, "Sit down," and she said, "I'm not going to sit down until I get my sweater," and I kept insisting that she sit down. So she said, "I'm not going to sit down." I said, "All right, then, keep standing, I don't care, but you're not going to leave the room to get your sweater *now*." So she kept standing and by that time the class was getting real unruly. There was giggling and there was talking; there were various spasmodic outbursts. Finally she sat down and as soon as she sat down I said, "All right, Denise, now you may get your sweater," and I let her go out and get her sweater.

In a sense it was a draw. I mean I gave in and I let her get the sweater, but at the same time she sat down first. So I didn't entirely lose the situation and I had some mastery over the situation in that at least I got her to sit down. I think under the circumstances I could have handled that a little more wisely now that I reflect on it. Number one, to these youngsters, money is probably hard to come by and losing a sweater could be a serious thing financially to this girl. If I hadn't been so harrassed and so confused, and if students hadn't been coming up to my desk so that I couldn't get settled, the chances are I would have said right then and there, "Go on Denise, get your sweater," but I was really in such a state myself that she was the straw that broke the camel's back. The way she ambled into class, just as breezy as you please, when the class period had started was one of the reasons that I was rather abrupt with her and said, "I don't want to hear about it, Denise, sit down." Then the class reacted with laughs, spasmodic giggles, and out and out rudeness. Fortunately I was able to get the girl at least to sit down so that she didn't completely defy me and get away with it. But at the same time, I did, what should I say, backtrack in the sense that I let her get her sweater.

I think this is probably a very important incident in that it shook me up a little. I felt that I had handled the situation unwisely and should have let her get her sweater promptly. However, I just couldn't give in, because then the class would know that anytime they wanted to do something, they would just have to insist and I would give in. If I wasn't so harried, I would have handled the situation a little differently, I'm sure. This way it was a close call, too close for comfort.

1. Do you agree with the teacher's evaluation of her own behavior?
2. Can you think of rules or regulations that could be established that would make such an incident unlikely? Why can you not just let teen-age students go in and out of the room on legitimate errands? Or could you?

3. Should students be required to obey any "command"?
4. Is it essential to have "perfect quiet" before you begin a lesson?
5. What do you think the teacher would have done if Denise did defy her and leave the room?
6. What might the teacher have done to grant the request and yet not "lose face"?
7. This teacher and many others have the notion that first you must get order in the classroom and then teach. Do you think the reverse might be true?
8. Is the fact that the teacher's desk was a mess important?
9. Would you think from the description that this teacher will "make it"?
10. How would you have handled the situation?

SUGGESTED READING

Ausubel, David P.:
"A Teaching Strategy for Culturally Deprived Pupils: Cognitive and Motivational Considerations,"
The School Review, vol. 71, pp. 458–463, Winter, 1963.
(Reprinted in Frost and Hawkes, *The Disadvantaged Child,* part V, chap. 29.)
Ausubel, David P.:
"A New Look at Classroom Discipline,"
Phi Delta Kappan, vol. 43, pp. 25–30, October, 1961.
Holbrook, David:
English for the Rejected,
Cambridge University Press, London, England, 1964.
Levine, Daniel A.:
"Differentiating Instruction for Disadvantaged Students,"
Educational Forum, vol. 30, no. 2, pp. 144–145, January, 1966.
Muus, Rolf:
First Aid for Classroom Discipline Problems,
Holt, Rinehart and Winston, Inc., New York, 1962.
Strom, Robert D. (ed.):
The Inner-city Classroom: Teacher Behaviors,
Charles Merrill Books, Inc., Columbus, Ohio, 1967.
(Sect. by Paul R. Hunt and Elvin I. Rasof:
"Discipline: Fun Class or Task?" pp. 131–145.)

Chapter Three
Continual Diagnosis and Planning

In the last chapter we noted that many discipline problems occur because of poor planning by the school or the teacher. Students may misbehave because they are asked to do something they cannot, or think they cannot, do. Frustration can cause feelings of inferiority and worthlessness, and the reaction may be one of avoidance or defiance.

How can a junior high school teacher be sure that what he is planning for the students is achievable? How does he know they have acquired the parcel of facts and the appropriate skills necessary to tackle the curriculum for his grade? According to the traditional grade system, if a child passed, he was supposed to be ready for the next year's work. Although all students were not expected to achieve at exactly the same rate or to reach the same precise level, there were usually specific requirements, called minimum essentials, that all were supposed to meet. This was especially true in the skill subjects. In the "olden days" the requirements were often as specific as "the ability to recite multiplication tables." Social studies mastery was difficult to appraise precisely, but even here a student usually had to pass a test (at 65 or 70 percent) which required memorization of a set number of facts and performance of certain skills, such as locating places on a map or identifying great men. As meager and inadequate as these standards were, it must be admitted that it was easier for a teacher to plan a program if he knew that most of the students who came to his grade had acquired certain skills and knowledge. Several events occurred that changed this neat picture. Educators finally became concerned about the large number of "left backs," students who often dropped out of school as soon as they could. It was also discovered that holding students in a grade two or three years did not always accomplish its purpose; repetition of the identical material in the same manner did not seem to be effective. Consequently, many school systems embarked on a policy of automatic promotion or some modification of it.

The rationalization for the automatic promotion policy stemmed chiefly from the mental hygiene movement which began to influence schools in the thirties. Certain studies as well as common sense observations by teachers showed that an overage boy often was made to feel ashamed when he remained with younger children. The effect of the failure caused a bitterness and resentment that made learning even more difficult for him than in the previous year. Also, schools formally acknowledged the fact that children of the same age do not all learn at the same rate. Special ungraded classes for the "mentally retarded" [1] had long been established, but little attention had been given to below-average normal children (70 to 90 IQ range) except to ask them to repeat the grade. As a consequence the new policy set up in many schools was to move children along with their age-group. In some schools the policy was to promote all students, in others to keep them back not more than one year. Consequently the achievement range within a class became even wider.

This range in achievement necessitated more individualization of instruction than most of the teachers had been taught to handle. In fact, they were often in a dilemma. The teacher was supposed to begin where the child was and still require him to complete the work of the *syllabus* for the new grade. In a few progressive schools, the curriculum for the skill subjects was planned so that each child could proceed at his own rate. Also, many elementary schools individualized to the extent of arranging for two or more reading groups in a room. By the time most students entered junior high, however, there was little provision for individuali-

[1] Usually those below 70 IQ.

zation, and a student might be placed in a class where all the textbooks were on a seventh-grade level even if he could not read at all. This problem was "met" by homogeneous grouping of classes. Not to get into the old controversy regarding the merits of homogeneous versus heterogeneous grouping, we need only say that even within any grouping system there is still some range of ability and some individualization is essential. Also we are concerned in this book chiefly with the students who are, according to all measures we now have, below grade level no matter how they are grouped. The big problem is what curriculum content should be required of these retarded students? For example, should the present seventh-grade curriculum be used as a framework but the content be watered down or cut? If it is decided to require fewer topics, the syllabus for the eighth grade will also need to be changed if it has as prerequisite the seventh-grade content. Should there be a separate and different curriculum all through school for the slower groups or should the whole graded system be abolished? The ungraded school would seem to be a possible solution, but traditions move like snails, and the *graded school system* is fraught with sentiment and vested interests. So even if the ungraded school should be the school of the future, it is unlikely that most cities will change their pattern within the next few years. When *you* begin to teach, you may:

1. Encounter fairly large classes grouped by IQ and/or reading level
2. Be given a syllabus and textbooks which will be beyond the ability of all but the top groups

Even *if* you are given appropriate materials, you will still need to find out for yourself the specific deficits of the class and of the individual children. You know now that many disadvantaged children have a limited vocabulary, faulty speech patterns, and difficulty in problem solving and abstract thinking. You know, too, that they may be emotionally immature and may act out in an unacceptable fashion. But if you are going to help them learn and progress, you will have to know more than these generalizations.

There are many formal and informal ways of learning about pupils in junior high school. Previous school records are available; standardized tests are given; parents and previous teachers can be consulted; community life can be observed; and the student himself can be formally interviewed. In the classroom, pretests and other teacher-made diagnostic instruments can be developed. Role playing, dramatization, and play activities which often reveal more subtle facets of the student's personality as well as academic abilities can be encouraged. Probably the most effective way is simple day-by-day observation by the teacher—listening carefully, asking questions, and encouraging students to ask them.

We shall now take up these various ways of becoming acquainted with the students' needs, interests, and abilities.

CONSULTING PREVIOUS RECORDS

Students usually come into a junior high or intermediate school from several different elementary schools. All elementary schools today provide cumulative records for the receiving school although some records are much more comprehensive than others. Usually standardized test scores, health data, attendance records, and report card marks are on each record. In the spaces marked "personality characteristics" or "social behavior" the remarks are usually meager and very subjective. Certain administrators ask teachers not to look at the records, fearing it will influence them to start out with a prejudice. It would seem, however, that if individual records are available, the teacher should take a quick look at them before he begins planning—if only to see the range of reading level if this has not been compiled as a class profile and made available to him. He does need to be sure before he issues the books that they are not all on a seventh-grade level if half of the students are reading on a fourth-grade level.

After the preliminary planning is done, the teacher will want to examine each child's record carefully. He will, of course, interpret subjective statements cautiously in terms of his own observations. He will note intelligence test scores and here again take into consideration the limitation of these tests and the fact that different instruments may have been used each year. At the end of the chapter you will find a copy of the elementary record of a boy who entered a junior high school. Such records are usually made available to the teachers unless confidential information is recorded.

STANDARDIZED TEST SCORES

In addition to the individual cumulative-record cards, the school office often makes up class frequency-distribution charts of standardized test scores. If these are not available, the teacher can make them himself from the individual scores. A summary sheet of reading scores can help him in planning for the total class. Below is a sample of data from three seventh-grade classes. Except for the lowest group, the students were not classified by ability. ⎯

FREQUENCY DISTRIBUTION OF
READING ACHIEVEMENT SCORES
Grade Equivalent Scores

Class	Below 3d	3d	4th	5th	6th	7th	8th	9th	10th	No. tested
7-1		6	5	3	7	1	1	2	2	27
7-2		3	6	7	4	4	2	3	—	29
7-3	6	15	7	—	—	—	—	—	—	28
Total	6	24	18	10	11	5	3	5	2	84

What problems do you think you might have in working with Groups 1 and 2? Why do certain educators feel that heterogeneous grouping should be preferred to grouping by ability? Why do most beginning teachers react negatively to having a wide range in one class?

The following is a reaction of a social studies teacher to working with these three groups:

Since 7-1 has a few bright students and a large slow group—with practically no average group—it is really creating problems. There is very little receptiveness and enthusiasm about work, because when the class is together, about half doesn't seem to be adjusted to the work level. I find that this has manifested itself in a need for changed lesson plans. I seem to have to vary simple questions and difficult questions; first one difficult and then one simple, so as to give the pupil of a different level the chance to bring himself out and to feel a part of the group. This has been very difficult for me because I've been used to running a lesson on one level; either a high level, a medium level, or a low level, and not varying the level of the lesson within each class. I find more variation is necessary. Perhaps a suggestion should be given to new teachers—that a lesson itself can't be on one level only; that within the lesson there must be an opportunity to move to various levels. The lesson may have map work in it for the pupils who have little understanding and also some concept questions for bright pupils, but this must be varied to give each of the pupils a feeling of participation.

I find that in 7-2 there are four or five youngsters who can't do the work I set up. The class is generally on a middle grade level. There are a few brighter ones, but most of them are on one level. This is a problem and it requires more differentiation of material than we are providing right now. I have discussed this with our coordinator. She agreed to use *Squanto*[2] with about half of 7-2. They will have less guidance than we gave to 7-3, who all are reading *Squanto*. They will also pick up the answer keys when they wish to and work by themselves most of the period, with just a short introduction at the beginning by the teacher. This introduction will last three or four minutes being a review of vocabulary and motivation for reading. I think this group will get a generally good experience with *Squanto*. I think it would be wise for me to concentrate mainly on the rest of the class, the brighter students, and really work on their level rather than beneath their level, which is what I think I've been doing for a certain amount of time.

[2] A. M. Anderson, *Squanto and the Pilgrims,* American Adventure Series, Row, Peterson & Company, Evanston, Ill., 1949. (This book was first used with a low seventh grade as a directed reading social studies project. It was very successful and later used as suggested reading with some of the children in the other classes.)

Achievement-test scores in subjects other than reading will also give the teacher a gross comparative picture of the degree of student knowledge in a particular content area. However, unless there is a classification of topics or an item analysis, the teacher will not find the rating too helpful in planning learning experiences. If he has copies of the tests and can make an item analysis, this may give him better leads. For example, a science teacher assumed that the children had a basic knowledge of magnets since this is "taught" in elementary grades, but the standardized science achievement test revealed that the items on magnets were missed by almost all the class. The teacher then decided to check by giving his own inventory and by setting up a lab situation in which he observed the students. He found that their understanding of magnets was meager. Consequently he planned to teach this material before moving to the topic in the syllabus.

TEACHER-MADE INSTRUMENTS

A teacher who is determined to begin where a child really is must be continuously alert to discover deficits and needs. There are the possibilities of both formal and informal interviews and just listening to casual conversations; teachers can also benefit from listening carefully to reactions during class activities and discussions, encouraging questioning, carefully observing work habits, checking assignments, and trying out a variety of new techniques.

Pretests

A social studies teacher who attempted to use a regular geography text with a very slow ninth grade discovered that the students had practically no knowledge of places in the United States and no map skills. In order to pinpoint the deficits, he devised a very simple test of basic information about places in the United States. Some of the findings were shocking to him. Only four of the twenty-three students could name as many as ten states. The majority could name only Florida, Texas, and New York. They listed countries and cities instead of states, e.g., Africa and Chicago. They did not know the difference between a country, city, or state. Few knew the names of the major oceans, rivers, or mountains. There was little indication of knowledge of geographic areas. When asked to name Western states, one child named *West* Hempstead, a New York suburb. Distance and time concepts were practically nonexistent. Boston was as far away from New York as California, and few knew how long it would take to get to any city in the United States.

It is not that these pieces of knowledge are necessarily the most essential facts for a thirteen-year-old student to know, but surely a teacher must *know* that the children *do not know* these things if he is trying to teach geography concepts that demand this background. Consequently such inventories or pretests will give the teacher information about the lack of basic or general information—information a teacher may take for granted when he begins teaching teen-age students.

This social studies teacher tried numerous ways of giving these youngsters some basic information about our country. While teaching these basic facts, he discovered additional deficits and also why some of these facts, which presumably had been taught in elementary school, did not stick or were never learned. He found that the "travel approach" so frequently used in elementary school and thought to be motivating did not appeal. The children did not seem to have any great desire to plan a make-believe trip to Wyoming. Perhaps they could see little chance of ever getting there. More successful were the simple games this teacher developed—naming states and locating them on the map, identifying cities by matching cards, etc. He was content at first if they learned only a very few facts. When they did learn a little about Detroit, Chicago, or San Francisco, it was amazing to note their growing interest when these places were referred to in current events or in stories which they were reading. They acquired a genuine satisfaction from recognizing places and being able to make some relevant comments.

Of more lasting importance perhaps was the effort the teacher made to develop certain concepts and relationships. He discovered from both the pretest and class discussion that the children were not able to estimate how long it would take to get to a certain place. He stated, "They would measure the distance from New York to California as 2,700 miles and when asked how long it would take to get there by plane, they said twelve hours. When I asked how this could be when they knew how fast a jet plane could now travel, they just looked blank. They could not make the connection until we went through several steps very slowly." Most disadvantaged children have inadequate time concepts, and when this is combined with only meager place knowledge, geography content is often meaningless. The same step-by-step process had to be employed to help these youngsters understand the relationship of a city to a state to a nation. Middle-class children acquire these concepts by an accretion of experiences. They travel and their parents describe activities going on in various cities so that they become aware of political entities almost without knowing it. Slum students often lack such experiences.

The pretest can be used in any subject area to determine background knowledge or skills. The teacher should make sure the children understand that they will not be graded on such a test but that it is given only to find out what to teach them or how to help them.

Children's Writing

The pretest, being a fairly structured quiz to find out whether students have specific information, has significant but limited value. It will tell the teacher whether or not students remember certain facts or can perform certain operations. However a less structured instrument may give him a better understanding of a child's deficits. It can reveal things that he had not thought to include in a pretest. English teachers often use students' themes or other written assignments not only to find out common errors in spelling and sentence structure but to get a better insight into a child's attitudes, beliefs, or feelings. Such information may be helpful in planning language experiences and in determining ways of trying to improve attitudes toward school. However certain children may refuse to write at all or write only one line. The reluctance to even try to write was overcome by some children when they were asked to talk into a tape recorder, then to hear the tape back, and to copy it down.

These following little paragraphs on "What I Would Do If I Won $1,000" told a teacher something about the differences in children's desires and feelings—their concepts of what $1,000 would buy—as well as their errors of spelling and grammar.

First I would stick myself with a needel to make sure I was not dreaming, then I would buy everything I wanted and take a trip to Paris and Haway. When I came back I would have nothing but the very best for my family.

If I won a thousand sollars I would use it for my college education. I have three reasons for wanting to put it away for college. (1) There will be no way of knowing wether or not I will have the amount of money when I need it. (2) It takes money to go to college. (3) and if I run out of money I will have enough to carry me through college.

The thing I would do is buy my mother a big luxry house. Give my brothers and sisters $25 every other week for allowance. Buy myself thousands of clothes, go to the beauty parlor every week that cost $50. With the leftovers I'd buy a bick, T.V., record player, typewriter, 50 records a week and last of all aparty every week.

I wood like to finish painting of the house for my brothers and I.

There will always be errors of punctuation, spelling, and sentence structure which are common to a large number of children. These errors can be attacked by planning a variety of drills and by concentrating on correcting them in future writing experiences. However, the teacher must be satisfied with a small amount of progress. Setting priorities and focusing on what he believes to be the most glaring mistakes or the ones that will handicap the children most is better than shooting at a dozen targets.

One teacher in analyzing the first writing attempts of her class found the most common spelling error to be the omission of the last consonant, particularly the "d," e.g., "die" for "died," "fine" for "find," "eren" for "errand." It was not only in connection with the past tense, as in "died" but whenever a "d" was the last letter, such as in "find." Such spelling errors are often the result of poor pronunciation; therefore the oral and written exercises have to be worked out together. Although this may seem like a minor matter compared with other deficits, it was a *concrete* problem that the teacher discovered and thought she could tackle. All through the year at intervals, the class played the "d" game, sang it, checked it, and teased each other about it. Improvement was evident. Other common errors of these children were confusion of "k" and "t," e.g., "strick" for "strict," "ack" for "act," and inability to distinguish vowels, e.g., "deslike" for "dislike," "tempur" for "temper," "nosie" for "noisy," "pint" for "paint," "met" for "meet." With this sort of *habit error* acquired through environment, learning *rules* for the past tense will not help, nor will teaching traditional phonics in a formal manner solve the problem. Having students listen carefully to their correct recordings and play games which focus on *particular* errors is more effective. Of course, if a teacher finds that there is some emotional resistance to these methods, he will discontinue them until the children are more at ease. But usually pupils do not mind these specific drills, and as far as spelling is concerned, the rewards are so immediate and concrete that they are often salutary. The teacher must be persistent however, perhaps saying, "I bet everyone will put the 'd's' on by June"; and each week in spelling and composition, he will total the mistakes. These are very simple diagnostic and planning devices. A teacher may also get help from the new curriculum materials which are linguistically based, but very often when he uses a prepared curriculum or a text without adequate diagnosis, he scatters his shots and accomplishes little. The speech and writing objectives should be set up in terms of specific goals. When given the suggestion for this kind of old-fashioned drill, a young teacher may remember that his college text played down or actually condemned "rote learning," repetitive drill, and an overemphasis on pronunciation and spelling. "You will stifle his creativity," the new teacher insists. "What difference does it make if he can't spell this word correctly?" Here we must admit that the Progressives may have been wrong. In trying to correct the meaningless and unnecessary drill that was often characteristic of the traditional elementary school, the "new" education stressed freedom and creativity. To be sure, when a teacher graded down a fine composition with two spelling errors, it discouraged a child and turned his focus on the less important aspect of creative writing. But to ignore the errors altogether is not helping the child either. With slow-learning children, there seems to be less resistance to drill than there is among brighter children. Ausubel [3] says that this is perhaps due to the fact that they *can* learn these tasks—which may be a simple repetition—without having to think abstractly or to figure something out. Also the task is concrete and immediately satisfying. "I got it right," says John. There should be, of course, time for students to imagine and create without being badgered about spelling and grammar. However, when a student begins to overcome his reluctance to write, a teacher can say, "This is fine but let's make it even better by correcting the errors." We should not underrate drills if they are based on needs, varied in type, and not pursued for too long a time period in one day.

Let Them Talk

Perhaps the best way to learn about children's strengths and weaknesses is to listen to them talk. Eavesdropping in

[3] David Ausubel, *The Psychology of Meaningful Verbal Learning*, Grune & Stratton, Inc., New York, 1963, p. 46.

the hall, playground, and classroom will be revealing to a teacher who is alert to a student's frustrations, fears, joys, and sorrows as well as to his interests, hobbies, and likes and dislikes about school. Making the classroom a place where students can talk freely without inhibition and yet not create bedlam takes time and patience. Here we are particularly concerned with the importance of discovering a child's academic deficits so that the teacher can plan appropriate learning experiences, and this can often be done by encouraging questioning during the class lessons.

During a reading period or a discussion, the student must feel free to ask about anything he does not understand, and the teacher must give a satisfying answer. The "look it up tonight" answer may work with a highly motivated student but not with the retarded child. He will probably not know how to look it up; he may not be able to find the material; or he may forget all about it. Eventually these students need to be taught to do research—deliberately and with a good deal of help—but the casual approach such as "Why don't you make a report on that?" is futile. If questions are answered on the spot or if a promise is given that they will be answered soon, the student will be content and will continue to ask questions, and the teacher will learn even more about what the child does *not* know, and can plan accordingly.

Because we think we know what students know and do not know, we are often surprised at the kind of deficits they have and at their concerns and interests. Below are listed some questions that surprised the teachers. The teachers had not thought to include these topics or bits of information in their prepared plans.

In a Lesson on Bones of the Body

"If bones are hard, how come we can bend over?" (had not understood about joints, etc.)
"Why don't some people have a bone in their nose?"
"What causes swelling?"
"Why is it if you get hit in a finger by a ball it hurts all the way up your arm?"

"If you sprain your ankle should you put it in hot or cold water?"

In a Lesson on the Heart

"If a man is paralyzed does his heart still beat?"
"If a man lies down still on a desert, will the hawk think he is dead and eat him?"

In a Lesson on Plant Life

"If a pistil gets pregnant how long does it take to develop? Is it nine days, nine weeks or nine months?"
"If everything needs exercise to grow how do plants get exercise?"

In a Lesson on Insurance

"If children die before parents who gets the insurance?"
"If a child is insured by parents does he have to pay it when he gets to be 21?"
"If a child is in an orphange after his parents die, will somebody pay his insurance?"
"If wife kills husband, will daughter get the insurance?"

In a Lesson on Qualifications for Voting

"Can the President vote in any state he wants?"

When reading stories aloud (a recommended practice for teaching poor readers), a teacher must not only answer questions but anticipate them. The common practice of assigning difficult words to be looked up before reading the story has little carry-over unless the context is explained by the teacher. However unless a teacher is very alert to deficits, he will often read entire passages thinking the children understand them when they do not. He must stop and ask questions and keep encouraging children to ask questions.

For example, children often think a word means what it sounds like—since they cannot spell. When asked the meaning of a "reef," a student replied that it was a Christmas "wreath." The teacher then encouraged him to work on context to see if he could guess the meaning of the word and then spelled out the two words on the board. Often a teacher takes for granted knowledge that children do not have, or they may have vague understanding but lack comprehension of precise meaning. A story about a hunt included the word "pheasants." The teacher thought the class would recognize the word since many came originally from rural areas of the South, but they did not recognize it. They tried to guess and some said "people" (confusing it with peasant), others said "an animal," and another, "a bird with a tail like a fan" (peacock). During this same discussion, the teacher realized that certain children used the words "fur" and "feathers" interchangeably and actually did not know the difference. Here again is the problem of the children not knowing precise meanings. How does a child learn fine differences—probably not by looking up definitions but by frequent encounter with words in conversations and in stories.

Another deficit of disadvantaged children is the lack of an understanding of symbols and metaphors. The ability to understand symbolic meaning is too often taken for granted. One teacher who discovered that her class was not familiar with commonly used expressions planned lessons in finding the meaning of very simple picture representations, such as the flag and the cross. She then moved on to more complex illustrations. The students liked finding symbols in their reading and making some up themselves. The same was true of metaphors and familiar quotations. They often volunteered expressions familiar to them that were not known to the teacher.

Dated or obsolete words are much less comprehensible to these children than to middle-class children who may have heard them at home or come across them in reading. A story entitled "Citronella Weather," which is included in an anthology commonly used in junior high schools, meant nothing to the class of seventh graders. It was interesting to note that the teacher assigned this story to students without discussing the meaning of the title.   She had not known what Citronella was herself but figured it out from the story and imagined the students would.[4]   Another story in the same anthology talked of a "toddler."   When asked how old a toddler was, the students had no idea, as this word was never used in their homes or neighborhoods.

Field Trips

Teachers can also find out much by taking children on trips.   Often the experiences are so new that the students learn little about the actual purpose for which the trip to a museum or historical spot is planned, but they still may learn a great deal about other things if the teacher is alert.   In our inner cities many of the students have not ventured far beyond their neighborhood.   The school trips are usually on buses and if the teacher does not pay attention to sights en route, he misses an opportunity.   If a teacher listens carefully to casual remarks, encourages questions, and points out interesting sights, he will learn a great deal about the children's paucity of information.   One teacher, when describing a trip on a ferry, told about how the students stayed very close to him because they were afraid to go up the gangplank.   When discussing the trip the next day, they remembered more about the people they had met than the places they had gone to.   They liked the man at the souvenir counter because he was nice to them.   For any *real* understanding of the historical places they had visited they needed not only more background information but more experience in just going places.

CONCLUSION

There are many ways of finding out about what students know and do not know and what they can do and cannot do.

---

[4] All readers under fifty may be curious.   Citronella was a patented name of a lotion for mosquito prevention.

General information can be obtained from their previous school records and from standardized tests. Other teachers and parents are another source. Information concerning specific lacks in knowledge and skills can be obtained by giving teacher-prepared pretests, encouraging student questions, analyzing their writing assignments, and just "listening in." A teacher then plans to try to make up these deficits, not all of them, of course, but those he deems most important. In the meantime he cannot demand performance of a job for which the child is not capable or for which he is not ready.

QUESTIONS FOR DISCUSSION

Read the following record and answer the questions on the following page.

ELEMENTARY SCHOOL RECORD

Jones, John   Class: 7–3

BORN: 7–26–48   Chronological Age: 13–7
RESIDENCE:
SIBLINGS: Older—1 brother, 1 sister
            Younger—1 brother, 3 sisters
      Lives with both parents in private house
      Father works
SCHOOL EXPERIENCE: Entered school 9/53
      Oak School—Kindergarten through Grade 5 (held
            over)
      Opportunity Class 5, 6

INTERVIEW INFORMATION:

6/57   Behavior problem and always on defensive. Dawdles to and from school.
6/58   Immature—Cries easily—However enjoys being teased and easily stops crying and holds no grudges.
6/59   Very immature. Cries readily.

11/59   Mother is glad boy is in opportunity class. Requests teacher train his temper. "Don't let him get away with anything. . . . Make him work. . . ."

6/60   William is much more controlled than in September. By next year he should be 100% better.

3/61   A dreadful fallback in work and conduct and control.

TEST DATA:

5/55	Pintner Cunningham Primary	IQ 84
3/57	Otis QS Alpha	IQ 88
10/60	Otis QS Beta	IQ 65
4/61	Metropolitan Intermediate Reading	W 3.7
4/61	Metropolitan Intermediate Arithmetic	R 3.2
		Comp. 2.5
		Prob. 3.8

SPECIAL ABILITIES: Arts, crafts
INTERESTS: Instrumental music, bike riding
GOALS: No plans

1. How valuable is this data to John's seventh-grade home-room teacher?
2. What additional data would you like to have if you were the teacher?
3. Suppose John is in your lowest group but that most of the other students read at least on a 4.5 level. What special provision might you need to make for him?
4. How might you try to find out whether the test scores are valid?
5. What would your first step be to try to help John?

SUGGESTED READING

Crow, Lester D., Walter I. Murray, and Hugh H. Smythe:
Educating the Culturally Disadvantaged Child,
David McKay Company, Inc., New York, 1966, chap. 5.
The Educationally Retarded and Disadvantaged,
The Sixty-sixth Yearbook of the National Society for the
Study of Education, edited by Paul A. Witty,
The University of Chicago Press, Chicago, 1967, chap. 5.
Passow, A. Harry, Miriam Goldberg, and Abraham J. Tannen-
baum (eds.):
Education of the Disadvantaged: A Book of Readings,
Holt, Rinehart and Winston, Inc., New York, 1967, chaps. 14,
18.
Storen, Helen F.:
"Making Up the Deficit,"
The Clearing House, vol. 39, no. 8, pp. 495–499, April, 1965.
Taba, Hilda, and Deborah Elkins:
Teaching Strategies for the Culturally Disadvantaged,
Rand McNally & Company, Chicago, 1966, chap. 3.

Chapter Four
What Content Will Appeal?

I n the last chapter we talked about making up the deficits which are reflected in standardized tests or school expectations. Certainly all the accumulated deficits of six years cannot be made up in the seventh grade, and for some children they can never be made up. However, where there are precise standards, such as those in the skill subjects, and teachers try to move students toward them, progress can be made even if it is slow. For example, the question of *selecting* content in mathematics is not a great problem because it is more or less set by the nature and structure of the subject (whether old math or new, there is a certain sequence of tasks).

In skill development it has been found that achievement satisfaction acts as sufficient motivation. If students can begin at the level they have reached and if they are helped to move toward achievable goals without too much frustration, they need little other motivation; nor is there any need to try to find out what aspect of the subject interests them most. They become interested in getting the right answer and in making progress. This same kind of motivation also often serves for spelling and certain reading skills. The aims are clear; the child knows where he is going; the assignment is definite; and the evaluation is concrete.

Selection of curriculum content in other subjects, such as social studies, science, and literature, is quite another matter. In addition to readiness, interest should play a dominant part in the choice. Since there is no generally agreed upon sequence in these subjects, school systems have developed various curriculum frameworks based upon rather dubious assumptions. About the only real guidelines are the time-honored ones that one must proceed usually from concrete to abstract and simple to complex. (However, educators do not seem to be able to agree concerning what is simple and what is complex.) The curriculum as it is set up in many junior high schools is not usually appropriate for disadvantaged youth. There are too many topics and too many abstract concepts. However, in some schools it is conceded that the teacher may modify the syllabus, and as long as he stays within a broad framework, he can do what he wants with the slow learners. Consequently it would be folly (although no one believes today that the *total* curriculum can be built solely on the interests of pupils) to ignore the *potency* of interest as one basis for selecting and organizing content. Teachers of disadvantaged adolescents seem to agree that there are some aspects of certain subject areas that have more appeal than others and that if the studies are focused in these directions, the students will have more desire to learn. When you begin to teach, you will have to keep your antennae ready to pick up new clues for selecting and organizing learning experiences. Nevertheless it may be helpful for you to know that we have found that disadvantaged students have a genuine and lively interest in personal relations, a fondness for fairy tales and folklore, and a preference for the biological aspects of science.

ABOUT PEOPLE

The Bridge teachers were all quick to sense the enthusiasm that emerged whenever the lessons related directly to people—what they looked like, how they felt about each other, why they were angry or afraid, and how they achieved success. The students would ask: "What did President X look like? Why did he do that? Did people have welfare in those days?" The interest would lag when the lesson moved into the mechanics of how a bill becomes a law or to the provisions of a treaty. All early adolescents are interested in people—especially themselves; but the middle-class student, academically oriented and conditioned by the time he reaches junior high school, has begun to be concerned about principles and to wrestle with abstract ideas. He has accepted the responsibility for learning about remote events and complex activities whether he is interested in them or not. This is not generally true of the slum child, whose intense concern with the personal aspects of any subject may be due to his lack of involvement with more remote current events. His life is lived in close "one-to-one" relationships. Teachers find little evidence that in the home there is much talk about broad political movements or events, community needs, or international affairs unless the family is immediately involved. In the Negro community during the past few years there has been a growing awareness of and concern for community action, if not always with the mechanics of legislation or the more complicated processes of social change. Students are becoming involved in mass movements. However, unless the parents are leaders, the students' greatest concerns are still focused on the personal day-to-day relationships.

These children have few hobbies. In the responses to a questionnaire given to junior high school students in slum areas, watching TV was the pupils' greatest leisure-time activity. They seldom built things, worked on models, collected things, or engaged in any other hobbies that might carry over to school content. Most of their leisure time was taken up with watching soap operas, reading scandal sheets, gossiping, hanging around, and trying to solve their own adolescent problems by talking to peers. The desire to carry over to the school the search for solutions to their personal problems should be capitalized on by selecting human relations content which is germane, but vicarious experiences may serve as a better approach than dealing directly with their problems. (Guidance or therapy sessions can be provided, but the regular subject teacher can contribute best perhaps by dealing more indirectly with personal problems.) As time goes on, the teachers can move children beyond their primitive, but very potent and necessary, desires and inter-

ests to the study of more complex social relationships and
to nonpersonal content.   Following are comments from the social studies teacher's
diary illustrating how he capitalized on the interest in people.

This class has had a rather extensive sub-unit on abolition.
We've found that using material with a *Biographical focus* is a
sure way to success.   The personalization of history would improve instruction in all schools, but it becomes more important
with this kind of youngster, for it makes for increased motivation and greater interest in the subject.   Since motivation is
really the key to learning in our situation, I find biographical
material highly useful.   The way we treated John Brown and the
raid at Harper's Ferry can be used as a case in point.   We used
a section of the poem by Stephen Vincent Benet, pictures, part
of a filmstrip, a dramatization, and text material for homework,
as well as the song sung by Paul Robeson to enrich the basic
material.   I find that when *varied* approaches are used, even
with the same personality, more students are reached by the
information.   The retention is greater.   We used materials rang-
ing from legal documents to articles in *Ebony Magazine* to create a feeling for and emotional involvement with the period we
were studying.   I found that the discussions regarding color
and race relations laid a firm foundation for the material that
was to come on Frederick Douglass.

I find that the students have tremendous interest in people.
They can relate their own problems to the characters in history.
In one class we read a biography, *Lincoln* by Anne Colver
(Scholastic Book Services).   They particularly liked the part
about Lincoln not being a perfect boy—the fact that he played
tricks on people.

I have presented current events in a manner this year different
from what I did last year.   I am assuming that the pupils' interest in people will make for greater interest in personalities than
in events.   We focus our discussions and our activities on
"Names in the News."   I find that greater understanding of the
events taking place results.   It gives the pupils security in reading the paper when they recognize names.   The classes are
much more news conscious this year than they were last year.
They discuss current events in an intelligent manner.   They

have a background upon which to base arguments or discussions.

One of the most successful projects during the first year of the Bridge Project was a unit in which the book *Squanto and the Pilgrims* was used as a basic text.[1] Written on a third-grade level but dealing with an adolescent boy, it was a superb choice. It had many exceedingly fruitful episodes in which human relations, especially appropriate for these children, could be explored. For example, as the book opens, Squanto is preparing for his initiation into his tribe. The question of how one demonstrates he is ready to assume an adult role in his society could easily and naturally be raised. In the latter part of the book Indian-white relationships occupy the center of attention. Squanto is enslaved, is taken to Europe, returns to America, and plays a critical role in the survival of the Pilgrims. These episodes offered opportunity to discuss personal and social problems. A similar sequence of lessons was developed using a biography of Frederick Douglass as the basic book.[2]

A biographical emphasis in history is not new, but in most schools it is used as a supplement rather than the essence. The student must read all about systems of government, treaties, and taxes in the regular text and then for a special report can read the life of a famous man. Why should it not be the other way around with the men and women the substance, and the events related to why the people made such laws and how they reacted to them? Another mistake that is often made is that teachers are afraid to make enough use of fiction. With reluctant junior high school learners it would seem wise to emphasize the drama of the events even if some

[1] A. M. Anderson, *Squanto and the Pilgrims,* American Adventure Series, Row, Peterson & Company, Evanston, Ill., 1949. (The book has become a classic for retarded adolescents. A description of its use appears also in Taba and Elkins, *Teaching Strategies for Culturally Disadvantaged.*)
[2] Robert W. Edgar and Carl Auria, *The Impact of Learning and Retention of Specially Developed History Materials for Culturally Deprived Children: An Exploratory Study,* Cooperative Research Small Contract Project no. S265, U.S. Office of Education, The Research Foundation of the City University of New York, 1966, p. 19.

of the facts are omitted or exaggerated.   Later there is time to correct and refine.   The most colorful periods of the persons' lives are the ones which will be remembered.   When reading the life of Frederick Douglass, the Bridge classes liked and understood his early life when he was escaping to freedom much better than his later life when he was developing organizations and making speeches.   A child remarked that she liked the life of Harriet Tubman much better than that of G. W. Carver because Harriet Tubman worked with people rather than plants.

One of the assumptions which was a basis for much of the curriculum material developed during the "Progressive era" was that the material should be related directly to the daily life of the child.   This corrective to the traditional social studies was taken too literally by teachers who tried to base a whole program on current life situations.   To be sure, students should have an opportunity to deal with their own immediate problems, but a direct attack is not always necessary.   It does not seem to matter whether the setting is near or far, past or present, as long as the students can understand the human relationships involved.   Vicarious experiences can increase understanding of their own lives without the teacher making it explicit.

Jerome Bruner makes a similar point:

I am sorry it is so difficult to say it clearly. What I am trying to say is that to personalize knowledge one does not simply liken it to the familiar. Rather one makes the familiar an instance of a more general case and thereby produces awareness of it. What the children were learning about was not seagulls and Eskimos, but about their own feelings and preconceptions that, up to then, were too implicit to be recognizable to them.[3]

But even material about people if devoid of action and feeling will not engender much enthusiasm.   A teacher from another inner-city school tells of her attempt to teach about the police department.

[3] Jerome S. Bruner, *Toward a Theory of Instruction,* Harvard University Press, Cambridge, Mass., 1960, p. 161.

My least successful lesson this week was with 7–15. The social studies book is geared for slow students and is more of a workbook than a text. This week our topic was the fire department and the police department in New York City. On the front sheet of the workbook there is an article about the police department and fire department, and on the reverse side there are questions (multiple choice, a match game and a fill-in.) At the end of the period, only one-third of the class had completed the assignment. I had asked them to read it silently and then answer the questions. However, when I saw they were having trouble I had some of it read aloud and I tried to explain parts of it and to let them ask questions. I thought I left time enough after our discussion for them to write the answers to the questions. However, many of them did not finish. They seemed to have no desire to do so and were uninterested in the questions in the book. While we were having discussions many of them had little stories they wanted to tell about the police department, and the incidents that they had with the police. They would raise their hands every other minute with the questions, if they couldn't understand something we had read together. Although the reaction was good because many of the children have had experience with the police department, not to say they were good experiences, but they wanted to talk about this rather than talk about the role of the police departments in our city which was explained in the text. I felt this was fine, but I also wanted them to know the role of the various departments in our city, and I felt that I wasn't getting this over because of their eagerness to present their little stories. So this lesson to me was not very successful. I don't think that I actually got over to them the role of the fire department or the police department and this was my main aim. Of course, I guess that they wanted to tell me the things that they understood best and those were the things that had involved them with the police not the role of the police department as described in the book. I was trying hard to get them to see the other sides of the picture, but I was not too successful and I didn't feel the lesson was successful at all.

This is a very clear-cut example of the teacher being determined that the children learn what was in the book instead of what they wanted to know. In this situation capitalizing on the students' daily lives would have been a natural and relevant approach. Many of the children had been involved with the police directly or indirectly. There was a good deal of hostility and criticism of the police department in the neighborhood.   School should surely be a good place to air some feelings and establish some facts.   Even without checking, one can easily guess the kind of anemic generalities that were contained in the workbook the students resisted.   No doubt it listed high-sounding democratic principles and briefly explained the broad functions and the organization of the police department.   Such generalizations could have been elicited after the students got answers to their own questions.   Much more successful was a teacher who was able to teach the methods of electing congressmen after the students had seen the two senatorial candidates when they came to campaign in their neighborhood.

Another case in point was a class reaction to a series of new booklets on outstanding members of minority groups. All the stories were about local people who had become successful, but frequently the content was meager and dull. "John studied very hard and won a scholarship," did not have nearly so much impact as the story about Lincoln's walking many miles to get a book and reading by candlelight. The highest criterion for selecting content is not time or place but the dramatic impact of the material.

In English classes, the Bridge teacher also found that material about people was responded to with more zest than essays and stories about nature.   The more feeling and drama in the story, the better. Fortunately, now one can even find mystery stories on a third-grade level.   Biography, if it contains exciting incidents, is as popular in English class as in social studies.   When commenting on the liking for biography, one of the English teachers reported:

For the past three days, I have been working on the culmination of my biography unit and this has made me very happy.   I made a series of cards with the names of the men and women the children had chosen to study and they had to match the name with the thing the person was famous for.   They enjoyed talking about how the times influenced what the people did.   They were fascinated in finding out about Copernicus and his theory that the earth traveled around the sun rather than vice-versa. They were very interested in Madame Curie, Magellan, and Ben Franklin. Many of the students did more than one report. From this we have written down a short passage on each person that everyone in the class reported on. And the class enjoyed it so much that instead of a one-day culmination we are going to have two. Another thing that I found interesting was that the children were eager to know what nationality the people were. For instance, they found out that Copernicus was Polish and Madame Curie was also Polish; Plato was Greek; Shakespeare was English. I felt that they showed a great deal of interest in other things outside themselves—far away things and other times. They asked all kinds of very perceptive questions; questions which indicate in every case that they are really thinking. And this makes me feel good, because these children really want to learn.

THE LAND OF MAKE-BELIEVE

Another interest almost as persistent as the curiosity about real people was the fascination of the make-believe. This comes as a shock to most new teachers who suppose that seventh graders are beyond the fairy-tale stage.

At the Bridge school we had many books available in the classroom including a large selection of the Scholastic paperbacks. The range was wide including simple classics, teen-age fiction, and stories written for very young children. Much to the surprise of the teachers the students quickly grabbed up the fairy tales.

The pupils love fairy tales and myths. They even like Rumpelstiltskin and the Oz books. When allowed to choose their own free reading books they often selected these. I think it was not only because they were easy to read, but because these children's emotional level is about that of a ten year old and consequently these books appeal. It may also be because their lives are rather dreary and they are starved for fantasy. The only children's classics that the pupils seemed to know were those they had seen on televsion or in the movies.

The teacher's conclusion may be right. It has often been said that a slum child's life is chaotic and that he is exposed to a certain amount of violence; his life is never boring. This is not entirely true, for although the slum child does often see "life in the raw," he also may have long hours of purposelessness and listlessness while parents work or are otherwise engaged. Many youths just hang around or sit by the television. A Cinderella hope exists in all of us—and if we were not fed some of these fancies at five or six years of age, perhaps we need them at thirteen.

Again, the conclusion about past and present being equally appealing was borne out in literature classes. Students liked both myths and legends.

One of the most successful things I've done to date was the American legends unit. All three classes loved it. They requested more and more legends so that I had to expand my plans from a week into a full-blown unit. The unit lasted six weeks and could have gone on longer. During that time the successful activities were: writing a composition on the legend they liked most; locating the legends we studied on a map; writing letters of request for a map of American legendary heroes put out by the Humble Oil Company; reading many legends; writing legends of our own about a hero we created; listening to folk songs on records telling about some of the heroes we had read about; singing musical legends together; and swapping legendary stories. Very few of the stories were disliked by the children. They seem to love fairy tale types of stories. While we were writing about legends, almost no one refused to write. The most popular heroes were John Henry, Paul Bunyan, Casey Jones, and Mr. Stormalong. It is interesting to note that when asked to write about the hero they thought the greatest, most of them picked John Henry. Also, the parts of that story they remembered best were—the gold-plated hammer, his giving it to Polly Anne, and the refrain, "He dies with his hammer in his hand." They loved singing the chorus of that song.

The interest in folklore diminished only when the story demanded a background of very complex or obtuse customs. The children had difficulty with some of the stories of Irish folklore that presupposed an understanding of certain local mores. One boy remarked that the only thing he remembered about an Irish tale was that the dying man kept "taking a swig out of the jug."

Surprisingly the outer space tales and other science fiction appealed only to the brightest of the students—probably because much of this reading demands technical knowledge. After these Bridge students had been exposed to science for two years and had acquired a background, more interest in science fiction developed.

THE HUMAN BODY

Another surefire topic of the Bridge students was anything about the human body. The reader may well ask, "Aren't all adolescents concerned with their physical needs and desires?" This is true, of course, but uneducated and impoverished families often lack even the most elementary medical knowledge. Their children have bits and pieces of information—much of it distorted, some of it completely false, and more than a little of it remnants of superstition. The pupils showed an intense desire to get information about all bodily functions, accidents, disease, pregnancy, alcoholism, dope addiction, and mental illness. They had not had any systematic study of these topics in the elementary school.

At the end of the three-year period, when asked on a questionnaire to list the topics they liked best in science, the greatest number of pupils listed "the human body." An end-term report of the science teacher included the following comments:

This year has been devoted mainly to the biological aspect of science. The major goal is to see ourselves as vibrant, healthy organisms performing functions necessary to living in our environment. We have included everything from the amoeba to humans with emphasis on physiology. We have shared common feelings when we studied the heart (how pulse quickens with excitement and how kidneys produce excessive urine when one is nervous or upset). We talked about adolescent moodiness, depression, and how all people shared these moods and how to overcome them. We learned about professions in the field of science, the different kinds of nurses and technicians. We found out how babies are conceived and born and were able to discuss these subjects without being silly or self-conscious. The questions were myriad regarding pregnancy and venereal disease. The children need and want to learn these things. Parents do not give them the information. Yes, I modified the curriculum. This seemed more important than "how nylon is made" so I spent more time in physiology than is usually done in junior high school.

Other excerpts from the science teacher's diary give specific examples of how she capitalized on the students' desires to know more about health and sickness.

Science has been a gentle probing into questions such as "How does our body work?" "What do different parts do?" "Why is it important to study about our bodies?" "Why is it important to study about disease and cleanliness?" There is no strict adhering to the syllabus. We discuss things generally and I try to answer as many questions as I can. Since most of our ninety children have an adequate social awareness, I capitalize on this and relate incidents where I can. I try to dispel superstitions where possible and talk about subjects most children *never discuss with adults,* viz.: V.D., birth, narcotics and alcohol—never preaching—only giving information.

They are asking some interesting questions about epilepsy, appendicitis, heart disease, diabetes, that make me think they are beginning to formulate good questions based on real desires for knowledge.

We have been studying the nervous system and I have chosen to concentrate on behavior. We have been discussing reflexes, both inborn and conditioned—and how we learn. I find the students are stating their basic anxieties, fears and frustrations. I assume that for most of them this is the first time they have discussed these things with an adult. Many wanted to know about temper tantrums and if they were normal. They found out that most adolescents share the same anxieties and that having moods is a part of growing up, but that too many extremes are signals for help. We discussed how to get this. When they referred to "crazy people," I explained mental illness. Many more discussions now take place and children are more willing to share with one another. They don't pick on each other as much.

The teacher's observations that the students prefer biological aspects to the physical and chemical topics in general science are supported by many others who have worked with this age-group. This teacher realized that the interest was due to normal adolescent needs. However, there may be a pedagogical reason as well for students to prefer biology to physics. Ausubel's explanation would seem reasonable.

The suggestion that sciences be studied in the order of their phenomenological complexity, i.e., that one start with the basic concepts of physics and chemistry before tackling the complex phenomena of biology and geology, although logically sound is psychologically unfeasible. More important pedagogically than the logical structure of knowledge is the pupils' intellectual readiness to handle different kinds of subject matter; and from the standpoint of relevant experience and readiness the phenomenologically "simple" laws of physics are far more abstract and difficult than the phenomenologically "complex" laws of biology and geology which are closer to everyday experience.[4]

CONCLUSION

In selecting and organizing learning experience, several criteria are usually applied. Final decisions for scope and sequence of subjects like social studies and science are usually made by "downtown" (in most cities, a central curriculum committee which may or may not have included teachers in the decision making), and whatever guidelines are used, the course of study that is often adopted for junior high schools does not always take into consideration the

[4] Ausubel, *The Psychology of Meaningful Verbal Learning,* Grune & Stratton, Inc., New York, 1963, p. 130.

fact that many students are not ready for this work. Consequently a teacher may be left on his own to modify or change the content. In many ways this is preferable to following the syllabus too closely, but it necessitates the teacher developing his own criteria. One criterion surely is immediate needs. If a child cannot read, he must be helped to do so; but even here there is the question of selecting reading material. *Interest,* then, can become one of the factors for selecting from the wide range of content in social studies and science. There is so much to learn. Why not pursue interests, which will act as motiviating devices for development of further and new interests?

The teachers in the Bridge Project, observing these adolescents for three years, discovered that the students enjoyed any material which dealt with the everyday lives of people—past or present—rather than topics dealing with movements or events where the people were obscure. Another category of high interest included fairy tales, fantasy, legends, and myths. This liking is probably related to the children's interest in people because after all there are human relationships in such stories even if they are not real; but it is conjectured that the interest also stems from the emotional immaturity of many of these children who may have missed the fairy-tale stage when they were younger. Again, related to the basic needs of all adolescents but more pronounced with disadvantaged children in large cities are concerns and curiosities about the human body, health, and sex.

To what extent such interests can and should be part of the curriculum depends upon many factors. An enthusiastic teacher can of course develop new interests, and he must try anything to see what takes. If he is alert, he will discover the sparks here and there and capitalize on them. The decision as to how exactly to structure the content and how much time to spend on a particular topic should be left to a teacher's good judgment. Is the students' curiosity about a specific area genuine and can it be satisfied by a simple short project or even a casual reply; or is the area such a fruitful one that at this time and place it should be developed into a unit or series of experiences? Should it be pursued by the total class, a small group, or an individual child? Does it seem to be a seminal topic—one for which there will be need for further explorations in the high school or in a vocation?

When a decision must be made as to how deep and how long a learning experience should be, again the teacher must use common sense. There are some aspects of a subject which must be learned very thoroughly, perhaps step by step. This kind of learning is essential in many walks of life. Everyone needs to learn a certain amount of patience and persistence and must pursue some things thoroughly. Parts of science content, according to our newest studies, need to be learned this way. But in literature surely it is sometimes good to just read a story without analyzing it and let the chips fall where they may. Most of the slow learners have never read a whole book. When they do, they consider it quite an achievement and do not wish to have to pull it to pieces. In social studies the question of wide or narrow attention to a topic may be determined by student ability and interest and relevance of the topic to the current society. Civil rights needs more attention from thirteen-year-olds today than tariff. A teacher has to play a little by ear in order to decide how long and how thoroughly a topic or problem should be pursued. Of course, all students should learn a few big concepts, which will transfer, but these need constantly to be concretized and must be experienced again and again if the concept is to be understood.

QUESTIONS FOR DISCUSSION

The following quotation comes from the recording of a teacher during her first month of teaching. The class is a seventh grade composed of thirty-five Negro and Puerto Rican pupils with reading levels from 3.7 to 4.9.

The Chamber of Commerce

My least successful lesson this week was a social studies lesson on the Chamber of Commerce. The thing that I think made this my least successful lesson was the discipline problem in the class. This class, 7–10, my one social studies class, which is also my official class, has some very difficult children in it. I have a problem in quieting that class down every time they come into the room. I get bad reports from all of their teachers. Their math teacher wrote on the section sheet, "Ernest and Robert were out of their seats, hitting people. The whole class was impossible." So this class has a reputation of being impossible, not that the whole class is that way but there are about six kids in there that are really sick, and I've read the confidentials on Ernest Brown, Robert James or Robert Smith (I'm not sure which is his name—he's listed on the record as Smith but his guardian's name is James and he calls himself James) and Sandra Mason. And anyway these children distract the class. Sandra has been better this week because I've spoken to her privately. The others I've spoken to privately but to no avail, really.

But getting back to the lesson, finally I managed to calm the class down and I had to send Ernest and Robert down to the dean in order to do it. And I had given them an assignment the night before to look up Chamber of Commerce. We're still without textbooks, so I told them if they couldn't find it at home in the dictionary they should try the library—ask the librarian what a Chamber of Commerce is, discuss it with their parents, discuss it with their friends, maybe somebody would be able to tell them. When they came into the room for "Do Now," once I had them quieted down I put on the board, "If you were a member of the Chamber of Commerce, what would you do to improve your community?" They all sat looking at me dumbfounded because half of them hadn't done their homework, so when I saw this look on their face—on their faces collectively—I told them to get out their notebooks with their homework and I was coming around to check it. I found that maybe half of the class did it. Some of them couldn't find the Chamber of Commerce anywhere, but they looked up the words chamber and commerce in the dictionary and they took their meanings. For chamber they found "an enclosure," and for commerce, "the buying and selling of commodities." So I tried to impress upon them that a Chamber of Commerce was an enclosure, it was composed of businessmen who do the buying and selling of commodities in the community, but this went completely over their heads unfortunately. I felt that this lesson was the most unsuccessful of the week because it went over their heads.   It was geared too high and they didn't have the appropriate reference material that they needed.   I just hope that I get the books quickly.

1. In the beginning Miss X says her lesson was unsuccessful because of poor discipline.   In the end she says it failed because it was above the heads of the children and they did not have the appropriate material.   Which of these reasons do you think is valid?
2. "The learning situation, to be of maximum value, must be perceived by the learner as realistic, meaningful and useful."[5]

   "The readiness attributable to particularized learning experience, also reflects the learner's specific educational history, i.e., his particular cognitive background."[6]

   The teacher realized too late that she had violated the above principles.   Why do you think that she did not know ahead of time that the children would not respond well to this topic?   If you felt you had to teach a topic for which children do not have an adequate background and interest, what would you do?
3. Homework assignments must be clear and specific. The task must be such that it can be completed in the time allotted.   Do you think the teacher herself could have found the meaning of "chamber of commerce" in the dictionary?   Do you think the children *tried* to find out the meaning from the library or from adults?   If they did try, why might they not have been able to get the answer?
4. When the teacher asked the children what they would do to improve the community if they were members of the chamber, she probably thought she was appealing to their interest by giving them a chance to say how

[5] William H. Burton, *The Guidance of Learning Activities,* Appleton-Century-Crofts, Inc., New York, 1962, p. 19.
[6] Ausubel, *op. cit.,* p. 30.

they would like to see things changed in the neighbor-hood. However, since they did not know the functions of the chamber of commerce, they could not answer the question. Even if they had known the meaning of the agency, do you think they would be genuinely interested in discussing the question?

5. If you found yourself in a situation where the children were not prepared for the lesson you had planned, what would you do?

SUGGESTED READING

The Educationally Retarded and Disadvantaged,
The Sixty-sixth Yearbook of the National Society for the Study of Education, edited by Paul A. Witty,
The University of Chicago Press, Chicago, 1967, chap. 9.

Elkins, Deborah:
Reading Improvement in the Junior High School,
Teachers College Press, Columbia University, New York, 1963.

Frost, Joe L., and Glenn R. Hawkes:
The Disadvantaged Child: Issues and Innovations,
Houghton Mifflin Company, Boston, 1966, part VI.

Jewett, Arno, Joseph Mersand, and Doris V. Gunderson (eds.):
Improving English Skills of Culturally Different Youth in Large Cities,
U.S. Office of Education, Washington, 1964.

Passow, A. Harry, Miriam Goldberg, and Abraham J. Tannen-baum (eds.):
Education of the Disadvantaged, A Book of Readings,
Holt, Rinehart and Winston, Inc., New York, 1967, chaps. 18, 22, 24–26.

Taba, Hilda, and Deborah Elkins:
Teaching Strategies for the Culturally Disadvantaged,
Rand McNally & Company, Chicago, 1966, chaps. 5–11.

Chapter Five
What Method Should I Use?

Any discussion of method cannot be separated from consideration of content and discipline since these are all interdependent aspects of teaching. Interesting, well-planned activities minimize behavior problems, and a particular method or technique should, of course, be selected in terms of the content goals as well as the pupils' ability and readiness. Examples of many kinds of approaches to learning have been cited in the previous chapters. This chapter will explore further ways that teachers may set about helping disadvantaged pupils achieve skills and develop understanding.

No one teaching procedure works effectively for every subject or for every class. In the past, educators have often made the mistake of overemphasizing a particular method, e.g., the developmental lessons, the activity unit, or the problem-solving approach. As previously stated, when a teacher plans to teach a body of subject matter, he must decide how much and how thoroughly his class should learn this subject. The fact that certain subjects, such as mathematics, must be learned rather precisely if a child is to proceed to the next step conditions the method as well as selection of content. At certain stages of the child's development literature may be taught chiefly for the story and at a later time for an appreciation of style. Before deciding upon method, the teacher must be sure of the goals. Is he trying to teach the children to memorize, analyze, discover, or just develop an interest or acquire a habit?

FLEXIBLE PLANNING

With slow or retarded students, a teacher must be especially flexible. He needs to set achievable goals in terms of the known needs of the students and to select appropriate activities, but he must be ready to shift from one style of teaching to another in response to the students' attention or lack of it. We are beginning to get new insights into the way children learn, but to date not much is available on the differences between the way (if there is a fundamental difference) the slow and bright children learn. Hilda Taba thinks that learning may be directly related to the amount of *concreteness* that is provided before any abstractions are attempted.[1] We also know that the attention span and degree of concentration of disadvantaged children are less than those of brighter children, which means that they may be unable to pursue a long or involved activity without a change of pace and without a good bit of guidance. Teachers soon discover that some of the less able students do not mind routine work—even rote learning—as much as able ones, but this does not mean that problem solving or critical thinking should not be encouraged. These children can think, but the activity must be meaningful, and the steps to arrive at a solution to a problem need to be many and taken at a slow pace. If the problem is too difficult, discouragement sets in and no learning can occur.

Since it is obviously not feasible, this short book cannot discuss all current controversies about learning theory or go into detail regarding all the teaching techniques which are included in a text on methods of instruction. The attempt will be made only to highlight some of the ways of teaching that teachers in deprived areas have found successful.

---

[1] Hilda Taba, Samuel Levine, and Elzay Freeman, *Thinking in Elementary School Children,* San Francisco State College, Cooperative Research Project, U.S. Office of Education No. 1574, 1965.

THE IMPORTANCE OF STRUCTURE

Most of the material written about the disadvantaged child makes a point of the importance of structuring the content as well as structuring classroom procedures which were discussed in Chapter 2.[2] A child who has had difficulty with learning needs to see where he is going. This does not conflict with the belief that the child also needs variety and some opportunity for freedom to explore. It does mean that when the teacher sets up a task, the goals and procedures must be clear. The teachers in the Bridge Project discovered that whether the activity was one of discussion, reporting, investigating, drilling, or evaluating, it must be clearly defined and well planned. A teacher may need to depart from his plan if the students' interests or needs demand it, but the departure must be conscious and the original plan modified, delayed, or discarded deliberately.

During the first few weeks of the Bridge Project the teachers found that their plans were too ambitious. One teacher reported:

I began to realize that I had set goals that were not attainable at this particular time. I expected too much of the children. I expected even more of myself and I found that I wasn't getting anything. I wasn't achieving much, though I was expending a great deal of energy. When I rewrote some of the lessons and I started to plan again, I began to realize that if I get one concept across then I have succeeded in teaching them something. I've learned to use material that will focus the attention of the students on a specific point and to avoid letting them wander all over the place. I think the students want and need very specific directions. In the Unit on the Revolutionary War I hope to keep the horizon wide but the road to it very narrow so the stu-

[2] For an interesting comment on the importance of structuring learning experiences see Daniel U. Levine, "Differentiating Instruction for Disadvantaged Students," *Educational Forum,* vol. 30, no. 2, pp. 143–147, January, 1966.

dents won't veer off the course.   In order to do this kind of work with the slowest group, it is best to begin with a structured, easy unit of work.   Gaining confidence is important both for teachers and students.   Work gradually with a few concepts and then introduce something new.   Keeping new learnings down to a minimum is extremely important.   Too many new things at one time lead to confusion with these children.

In another class where children were given short daily assignments with provision for the more able to move at their own rate, the teacher also saw the importance of structure.

There have been first signs of success with the 7–3 class and I will have to admit that this success comes as a result of the Squanto material.   Because of the kids' earnest desire to get involved with the material, they were more willing to quiet down and to listen.   Previously, because of my lack of experience in selecting appropriate material and in giving clear directions, they were not eager to get started each day.   Now, because they genuinely enjoy Squanto and because the lessons are more structured, they begin to work at once.   They give out the papers and books when it is necessary and they collect them. They know where they are going and they have developed a sense of responsibility.

These two examples show the teacher found success when he selected material the students were ready to master and organized it to facilitate sequential learning.

Educators may be somewhat responsible for the underrating of structure.   In the Progressives' criticism of traditional methods of teaching facts, they often cited the most flagrant abuses, implying that structure is tantamount to meaningless rote learning, whereas it is essential to a basic understanding of concepts and principles.   Ausubel says it nicely:

The art and science of presenting ideas and information meaningfully and effectively—so that clear stable and unambiguous meanings emerge and are retained over a long period of time as an organized body of knowledge is really the principal function of pedagogy.   This is a demanding and creative task rather than a routine or mechanical one. The job of selecting, organizing, presenting and translating subject matter content in a developmentally appropriate manner requires more than a rote listing of facts. If it is done properly it is the work of a master teacher and is hardly to be disdained.[3]

THE "SATURATION" APPROACH

In addition to structure, the Bridge teachers cited what they considered to be another essential for helping pupils acquire knowledge. They called this the "saturation" technique. It was found that "once-over-lightly" teaching did not work with disadvantaged children if the material was to have any impact./The pupils needed more repetition, more explanation, and more connecting links than other children needed. Since simple repetition of the same exercise would become boring and attention would lag, it was necessary to plan to present material in a variety of ways. / Several approaches were sometimes used to develop one central concept or skill. Following are examples of attempts to make the subject matter stick:

In my teaching I have subscribed to the theory that our pupils need something repeated in as many meaningful ways as possible. One case in point is the way we treated the teaching of the death of Franklin Delano Roosevelt. In addition to reading the text, newspaper accounts were used. We looked through the pictures that had been printed in *Life* magazine at the time. We read accounts in the book *When F. D. R. Died* by Bernard Asabell. We listened to an Arthur Godfrey recording of the funeral. Pupils read easy biographies of his life. Class discussions were held comparing the death of Roosevelt with the death of Abraham Lincoln. Comparisons were made of the situation in which each occurred. In the brightest class a discussion was held debating the big "if" in history. How might history have been changed if neither of these men had died when they did?

[3] Ausubel, *The Psychology of Meaningful Verbal Learning,* Grune & Stratton, Inc., New York, 1963, p. 19.

Another example illustrates the way the teacher tried to repeat main ideas in different contexts and also used visual aids to make meanings clear.

The third part of the Unit on industry was perhaps the most successful. We spent a great deal of time on steel, using many kinds of materials. Initially we used the *World of Steel* published by United States Steel. This is an extremely useful booklet, describing the uses and production of steel. We used the filmstrip, "The Making of Steel." This enabled the pupils to visualize things that they had only heard about. I had samples of steel and its raw materials which were shown and used. The pupils were shown pictures and they made their own special bulletin board in the hall. They used the text for some of the factual material. They read a story, "The Open Hearth," to lend some of the human drama of the steel mill to the unit. The pupils made maps to trace the route followed in securing the raw materials for steel. This is merely the pattern that was set for further study in this important area. We tried to vary materials as much as possible and to make them as meaningful as possible and I think that this enhanced learning. The classes responded well to the work.

The teachers agreed that in all classes they needed to help the children develop the ability to remember and that even in literature they could not just run through a story as quickly as they might with more able students. Most of the children had not read books of any length; and since they were able to read only a few pages each day, the English teacher tried various ways of helping them get full measure from a story while making sure that it was thoroughly understood as well as enjoyed. When teaching *Blue Willow*,[4] one teacher used the following techniques:

1. Children retelling the story
2. Listening to small sections read at a time and ending on some crucial moment
3. Answering questions rexographed for every day of the reading

[4] Doris Gates, *Blue Willow,* The Viking Press, Inc., New York, 1940, and also Scholastic Book Service, 1960.

4. Writing radio plays from the dialogue in the book
5. Acting out the scripts
6. Taping the performance of scripts
7. Listening to the tapes
8. Viewing photographs of the background of the story
9. Writing composition exploring the social relationships of the leading characters

This teacher reported in her diary,

The children anxiously look forward to anything related to the scripts: their rehearsal, performance, tapes. At first I tried working without daily rexographed comprehension sheets, but without these exercises the children did not always read the chapters carefully. They seemed to need a sense of daily accomplishment, so I prepared daily work sheets for them. The scripts continued to provide the necessary variation of activity and sparked interest in the material. I feel that the retention of this material resulted from three all-important principles which will guide all my work with the extremely slow classes in the future:

a. Provide interesting, varied activities daily on the same material.
b. Repeat the same material over a long period of time in many different ways. Use a long project made of short, satisfying pieces (my Unit lasted almost eight weeks).
c. Give daily short writing periods that conclude the lesson in some way (summary statement, answers to questions, radio scripts, etc.) thereby giving the children the feeling of a day spent in finishing a project that is worthwhile, a sense of accomplishment.

The "saturation" approach for each unit was supplemented by informally referring back to unit content throughout the year. The teachers found that they had to use every opportunity to help students recall the facts and concepts that they had already taught. Teachers' comments like the following were often heard in the classrooms:

Remember, we had that word in last week's story.

Come to the map and find Boston.   We found it when we studied about the Revolution, remember.

Who can help us remember how we set up the experiment for staining slides?

This kind of periodic review is much more effective than the formal review periods each day or week which are often used in traditional classrooms.

DISCUSSION TECHNIQUES

The most common method of teaching in the majority of schools is called "discussion," but more frequently than not it turns out to be a recitation or a simple question-and-answer procedure following a reading assignment.   This method is extremely time consuming and seldom holds the interest or attention of anyone but the student who is being called on. With the kind of child we are describing, this method is usually unrewarding to both teacher and pupil.   Occasionally a spell down or quiz-type recitation may stimulate children to learn a specific kind of information, but the kind and variety of learning experiences just described above under "The Saturation Approach" are, as a rule, much more effective than the daily recitation lessons. However, genuine discussion or "talking about" a topic or a problem does provide opportunity for clarification, enrichment, and student questioning.   It is *one* way to learn, and should be included in the spectrum of possible activities.   A major need of disadvantaged students is to learn to express themselves in more than one-word replies and to be able to get joy as well as knowledge from exchanging information and ideas.   Guided discussion can contribute to this goal.

To provide for discussion experiences, an English teacher in the Bridge Project used many approaches.   The interview technique was used during the first week of school to help students get acquainted.

In preparation for interviewing each other, I had one student in each class interview *me*.   In class 7-1, there was an excellent interview done by Lawrence who volunteered his services.   The class response was excellent and there was much good humor. Lawrence was very capable of speaking with an adult and seemed very relaxed and at ease. In 7-2, the interview was done by Sheila who didn't know how to speak with an adult at all. She didn't know where to begin or how to conduct herself and was exceedingly nervous, even though she had volunteered to do the interview.

In 7-3, the response was exactly the same with Richard doing the interview. From this I realized that these children can't speak with adults at all. They don't know anything about the art of conversation. One word is all they give in answer to any question in oral communication. Several of the students from 7-1, however, are just the opposite. They are very poised, confident and verbal.

Pairs of pupils interview each other following the set of questions that we developed together. They wanted to know what their favorite TV programs were, what movie stars they liked, what school they had gone to before, how many children were in the family. They lost some of their shyness and enjoyed the activity. After the interview they wrote up their findings.

Here you can see the difference between the highest and lowest of the teacher's three classes of the seventh grade. Although the results were rather dismal in the lowest groups, as more opportunity for informal discussion was provided the students became more verbal and less self-conscious. When these children were in the eighth grade, the teacher made the following comments:

One of the main parts of the English program is discussion. Every class period has some time for discussion. Generally the children talk about the concepts in their reading. At other times pupils read their work to the class and others evaluate what they have done. At still other times children propose to the class plans that they have thought about, and the rest tell what they think about them. As a whole, I think the children are better able to express their thoughts than they have ever been. Surely they express themselves more clearly and more to the point than ever before, even if it's still not grammatically correct.

In the lowest class the discussion is usually limited to a very short time. They respond well to such questions as "Would you consider Lupe and Janey brave? Why?" To compensate for their inability to handle lengthy discussions they do more reading aloud, answering direct questions through the lesson, and act out many more plays. Their talking is always based on something concrete. Rarely do they express abstractions and they must be helped to draw conclusions. Even if 8–3 is studying the same material as the other two classes, the handling of it is different. For example, in the American Legends Unit the same legends were read in all three classes. I did more of the reading in 8-3; they had listening sheets to fill out. When they did the reading, they concentrated on the story line. With 8-1 and 8-2 we were able to discuss such concepts as—*man needs heroic figures to look up to, different regions need different kinds of heroes.*

When trying to hold discussions in social studies classes, the teacher had a difficult time during the first year of the project. He found that many students were afraid to compete in the discussion of a topic because they were neither as well prepared nor as verbal as a few members of the class. Those who had more knowledge of the topic all talked at once and seemed to have little control. Many teachers find it difficult to teach discussion techniques to any children of this age-group, but it is even more difficult to teach deprived children. The students have less self-control, less practice in the social amenities, and less genuine confidence than middle-class children. As a result, the teacher, after some unsuccessful attempts, backtracked from the free discussion and set a more formal procedure: listing subtopics, making sure preparation was adequate, and working out ground rules. With the lowest group, he tended to read aloud more, which the children loved, let them ask questions as they went along, and limited the discussion to about ten or fifteen minutes.

Discussion improved when the topic could be related to direct experience. The teacher wrote in his diary during the second year:

In teaching history during the last quarter, it was my primary aim not so much to teach the facts as to create the feelings

that were experienced by our fathers and grandfathers . . .
What happened in my father's teen years? What was the world
like then? How did they feel about Hitler, Mussolini, and Sta-
lin? Here we had tremendous human resources in experience
to fall back upon. The children brought in accounts of conversations they had had with their parents. This was one of the
few times that I've heard of conversations that our pupils had
had with their parents.

I noticed that the pupils started to compete with each other.
After a few days, more and more pupils were responding to the
experience questions that were being thrown out. The pupils
were told, "Ask your parents and neighbors what hardships
they had to endure during the depression." The next day the
pupils came in with all kinds of stories about life in depression
times. It was meaningless for them to read in the text that the
country people were better off than those who lived in the city,
but it was only during a class discussion in which parental
experiences came out that we were actually able to determine
the reasons it was preferable to live on a farm or in the country
during the '30's. This has really opened up a whole new area
of thought for me. I think that one of the problems that we face
in South Jamaica is that there is a noninvolvement of the
parents in the school of the children. I remember when I went
to school the work that I studied during the day was often the
topic of conversation at the dinner table. I think that often
when our pupils take home knowledge it is meaningless for the
parents, but when these parents are able to relate experiences
that otherwise might remain unmentioned, this serves a dual
purpose. It enables the child to get closer to the parents and
provides for a useful family exchange whereby all can benefit.
It also lends realism and depth to the learning and ties together
the school and the home. I hope to enlarge upon this next
year.

Toward the beginning of the third year all three teachers reported progress.

I have found that many of the pupils now like communicating
ideas to each other, but in the beginning they didn't know how
to do this well and it was a strain for them. Initially they
rejected it. They often felt uncomfortable in a discussion and
therefore tuned out—not at all happy at the fact that they were

tuning out, but doing it as a protection in a way.   I find now the students have more confidence in expressing themselves in front of a group.   They are more willing to participate.   They feel better for it.   They get a feeling of satisfaction after a successful discussion.   They will refer back to it for days.   Some children who had always been loners began to participate in the group work.   Now when the research is completed on a topic and the groups report their findings, the children really listen to each other.

DRAMATIZATION

Another successful procedure with disadvantaged pupils is dramatization.   It appeals particularly to the young adolescents who are not yet as self-conscious as they will become in the senior high school.

The English teacher in the Bridge Project provided much opportunity for acting.   Sometimes the pupils took exact dialogue from a story and acted out a dramatic incident; other times they wrote play material themselves.   These activities were intended to develop assurance and poise, and here the teacher gradually began to stress correct and effective speaking.   Often the children tape-recorded their dramatizations, and they loved hearing their own voices.

Probably the most successful thing I have done with 8-3 is to have them write sections of a story into a play, rehearse it, and then act it out with the tape recorder taking it all down.   I was petrified to try it at first.   I had half the class complete the writing of the script while the others were seated in a circle in another part of the room rehearsing.   (I called the coordinator in to be prepared in case of any uprising.)   Everyone worked extremely well.   They ask me almost every time they walk into the room, "Can we act out a part of the book today?"   Naturally this is one of the activities I will use often.

"Role playing" also has multiple values.   It often reveals hidden feelings which are not overtly evident.   But simply as an exercise to develop spontaneous expression, it is also worthwhile.   The mistake that teachers often make is to try to get students to imagine situations which they really have no background for, and hence they portray only generalities which have little vigor or meaning. This happens sometimes when uninformed youngsters are asked to act like an historical personage or a modern diplomat. However, if the content is familiar or if the situation is a simple and universal one, role playing can be an excellent learning activity. Students in one class enjoyed playing the part of a colonist selecting people to come with him to America in the seventeenth century. Not only did they see the need for various kinds of farmers, artisans, and tradesmen, but they discussed the kind of personalities that might succeed in the New World and have the courage and perseverance to stick it out.

GROUP WORK

Long units which demand sustained research by committees are not possible for most of these children. However the Bridge teachers tried various ways of having the classes work in small groups on short assignments, and eventually a few longer group projects were carried out. The greatest problem the teachers faced was trying to give enough attention to each group during the work phase of the activity. Children wanted the teacher's attention every minute, and of course there were always a few who took advantage of the freedom and wandered out into the hall. One teacher reported:

In the newspaper unit I've divided the class into groups of from four to six pupils and they move their chairs and desks to work on these units. For instance, we have the fashion group, the editorial staff group, and so on. The first time we did it, it worked beautifully with 8-1. Incidentally, we work as an entire class. 8-2 presented more problems. For example, there was the day when Clarence got his bloody nose from being punched by David. Because of working in groups, and my working with one group at a time, my back was turned toward the door of the room and David had the opportunity to sneak out and be out in the halls without my knowledge. And this turned into quite a news item in school and caused several people to warn me not to work in groups again. Nevertheless, the following day I divided the class into groups again. But it does show the hazards of group work and I certainly learned a lot from this experience. I'd better keep my back facing the other end of the room and keep my eye near the door so that no one can come wandering in and out.

The next example shows how important it is to give careful directions and to help the students make a plan and keep a progress report.

As a result of the success with taping of dialogue during the reading of the two novels, I judged correctly that an enjoyable and profitable unit would be a theatre unit. My expectations were more than realized in the eight weeks the unit lasted.
The longest activity of the unit was the work leading up to the final presentation of two plays by each class. Each class was divided into groups working independently on their own plays, to be presented at the end of the unit. The children selected the play they wished to be in. At the first group meeting, they chose a group leader (director) and a secretary. The secretary's job was to take minutes and fill in the activities chart I rexographed for them. For each date they listed what progress they had made. After the first day, the group leader took over his job and I acted only as an advisor or consultant. The most important result of this set-up was that the children learned to work well together independently. They had a job to do and were anxious to complete it. The children cooperated with their leaders and fellow group members. They really worked together as teams.
Of the six acting companies, only one was unable to meet the performance deadline date. As a result, they had to admit they were unable to perform. Said the various children in the group: "We should have elected a stronger leader, someone who would make us work." "The other groups are so well-organized." "We don't get anything done because we don't work together," and so forth.
The non-performing group was bitter about not performing. They were ashamed they couldn't do better together. I think they learned just as much, or more, by not meeting the standards than the other groups did by finishing their plays.

In order to provide for individual needs and at the same time teach the students to work together and help each other, the mathematics teacher devised the following arrangement:

I've been breaking the classes up into groups of four. I've done it randomly, so that the children who are not so bright don't feel badly. (I have heard some of them say, "Oh, I'm stupid compared to Valerie," or "I'm stupid compared to Dan.") So I seated them in groups of four and gave them differentiated math material. During the period each child had to finish a certain number of problems. I asked them to work and to test each other. It has worked wonders. The children seem to be learning. I see John helping Jack and being very patient with him, and I find I can spend at least five or ten minutes with each group going over their particular problems. If I teach one concept like division of fractions, I teach it to the entire class. Then I break them up into groups and they work problems. I have one group creating original problems and putting them on the board. And the other groups answer them.

I have one class which includes Priscila, Madeline, Leonard, and Harold who are very, very slow, do not read well and do not comprehend, and this makes it difficult to teach the entire class the same lesson. I tend to focus on the brighter child, which I know is wrong, but I do this anyway. However when I tried the group work in this class, it worked very well. The only modification I made is that I put one brighter child in each group, and I call him the *Help Person*. He is there to help the others. Now he doesn't feel bored because he is busy explaining and the other children are learning. When they can't understand something, I walk over and I help them. I don't do this every day. I do it once or twice a week, and so far it is working very nicely. I am keeping very good notes on this so I will have a picture of this at the end of the term. I am also giving them a test on Tuesday of this week and I will see how they do. I am making up different tests for each group. Then I plan to give each child a series of topics that he is to cover in a certain amount of time. This needs further planning and we are doing this now.

It took careful planning, continuous guidance, and infinite patience to teach these pupils to work together. By the ninth grade the children had greatly improved their group-work skills.   In a unit on occupations, the teacher reported:

The children then broke up into groups or worked by them-selves on the research.   They got their information largely from the booklets which we had obtained from the New York Life Insurance Co. and other sources.   I think the group work was successful because children with the same interests could share the work load, give each other information and share their own impressions and feelings in regard to their occupational choice. Some children who had always been loners before actively par-ticipated in the group work.   When the research had been com-pleted, each group gave a report of its findings.   Again I was amazed to find the children really listening to each other and they learned a great deal about most well-known occupations. When each group had reported, they were to put their findings in a job chart which covered the whole back wall.

Again, the lowest class had the most difficulty working to-gether.   Cooperation was hard and there was resentment of student   direction   and   leadership.   Gradually   they,   too, learned and were able to plan and work together without fighting.   During the last semester of the project, the science teacher gave this touching example:

I found that few children were able to identify any of the flowers I brought to school.   What further amazed me is that they knew nothing about seed plants.   Here again I had assumed that many had experienced the growing of plants since they had little houses or had visited down south.   They did know about cotton, but did not realize that cotton plants came from seeds. In their minds there was little or no connection between the seeds of a tomato and the plant itself.
    We used a textbook entitled *Your Biology* (Harcourt, Brace & World) a 7th grade book which the school purchased for the new curriculum.   The book has excellent illustrations and many good reading selections.   The children liked the book and asked to use it.   We used this as our guide.
    As we worked at identifying seed plants and discussing the many varieties, I asked how many had actually ever planted a garden.   Out of 22 present, only 7 youngsters raised their hands.

Barbara knew about plants and was happy to share her knowledge.

After we talked about them and discussed vegetables and flowers, I asked how many wanted to plant their own seeds. All but Leonard, William and John wanted to. These said, "That's baby-stuff." Charles organized the planting. We had soil, pots and radish and pea seeds. Barbara advised the group (18 up at the front table) how to plant by reading the instructions on the seed packages. Charles divided the soil and Linda placed blotters on each hole in the bottom of the pots.

I was in the background. As I watched I was happy at the fact that they functioned so well as a group—no quarrels—no name calling. Most of all, they were having fun. I was sad, too, to think how physically grown they are and how emotionally young they are—inexperienced individuals trying desperately to cope with the world. It saddened me more to think of the childhood pleasures so many of them have missed and how they need to experience so much of these elementary activities when they are young. They are all grown up physically, and so young emotionally.

Each child had planted his own seeds. By the time we were finished, Charles had each pot labeled and the children were writing in their diaries what they had done. There was talk about planting and how wonderful it is to get so many different vegetables and plants from seeds. We recalled the story of *Johnny Appleseed* and the children all agreed it was really good. That afternoon we came back to homeroom early and Cheryl, who was out in the morning, asked me if she could plant her seeds. Leonard and William, who thought it was kid stuff, asked, too. While the others checked to see if their plants were all right, Charles aided Cheryl, Lennie, and William.

From these examples we can see that structure is just as important in small-group work as in total class or individual activities—perhaps even more so. In the beginning very specific directions are necessary, and even then there is bound to be a certain amount of confusion. The teacher cannot become discouraged if resentments come to the surface or if there is a refusal to listen to others and a reluctance to share. For many students, working together seems to be a new experience. In school systems where this kind of activity is learned well in elementary school there are fewer problems.   However the young adolescent tends to be an ambivalent creature, wanting to excel and to boss one minute and to conform at another—all these characteristics are magnified when he is put into a group.   The Bridge teachers had three years to work with their children and gradually helped them to achieve a certain amount of respect for others and to gain the ability to experience satisfaction from a group activity.

INSTRUCTIONAL MATERIALS

A discussion of method must, of course, include some mention of materials.   Many of the examples given here have made specific reference to the kind of materials used.   We noted too that young teachers continually complain of the lack of appropriate materials for slow learners.   This lack is being rapidly remedied, and makes us wonder if the commercial materials will begin to control the curriculum for the disadvantaged classes as the "Regents Review Books" have often dictated the content of a college-preparatory course. The skillful teacher makes his own plans and selects material from whatever appropriate source will help achieve his goals.

Use of the Textbook

The most widely used instructional matter in the United States is the textbook.   Usually a single set of grade-level texts is provided for each class.   For the beginning teacher a text does give a certain sense of security, and if the book is an appropriate one, the teacher may depend upon it until he is able to select and organize other materials.   But if the textbook is above the reading level of the majority of students, the teacher cannot simply assign the lessons and expect comprehension.

Below is an account of how a teacher used a text which was above the students' reading ability.   Obviously such a situation should not occur, and teachers soon will learn to get more appropriate material by hook or crook, but in an emergency this kind of modification made use of the book possible.

Example: *Lessons on Static Electricity*
            pp. 342–348 *Science for Progress*
            (a regular junior high school text).
Class 9–6 (Median reading level–4.5)–
1. First we will review concepts already learned concerning static electricity.
2. We will then develop the meaning of static.
3. Recall the work of Benjamin Franklin and his kite incident.
4. Review our knowledge of negative and positive charges. We can then talk about the words directly related to the reading: "shuffled," "shock," "charges," "electrified," "negative" and "positive."
5. We look carefully at the pictures and recall the demonstrations we did in class.
6. We are then ready to read the paragraph silently, and then aloud.
7. P. 342—to the top of P. 343.
8. We then discuss the repelling and attracting ability of charges. Which pictures on the page show this to be true? What signs show negative? What signs show positive?
9. Read the paragraph "Like Charges Repel; Unlike Attract."
10. The paragraph on electrons is a little too advanced. We might skip that and go on with "Insulators and Conductors" and this can be extended or shortened depending on the time available.

The adaptations are not complete but give some idea of what can be done. Unfortunately all topics are not handled with ease (in the teaching or the reading). It would be much easier if there were elementary school science books without a grade designation for classes. If a teacher had nerve, he could withhold texts until parents asked for them, and then the parents would know there were not any appropriate books available.

It takes a lot of hard work and patience to adapt the material for slow readers. Often it is easier to do without the book.

This is especially true when a teacher has never had any training in this type of work.

Before commenting on other ways of using textbooks, a word might be said about disadvantaged children's attitudes toward textbooks. Because a text is a *symbol* of learning and is used so extensively and often exclusively, students seem to attach a prestige label to it and give it significance far beyond its worth. Slow students have often remarked that it is not learning when they read from a trade book or watch a film. Parents also *want* children to have a text. Although in time children, and even parents, can be weaned away from this distorted notion, it does no harm to cater to it in the beginning. Consequently teachers often assign a textbook to each child, if this has been school policy, even though they may not intend to use it regularly.

If it is a good text on the appropriate reading level, a new teacher may well rely on it for at least part of his classwork. However, he will soon discover, if he did not know before, that even the best texts are inadequate. No able teacher can long endure letting the textbook be the sole guide for his teaching. His own ideas and the particular deficiencies and desires of the children will soon challenge him to plan units and lessons carefully, using the text *only as he chooses* to achieve his objectives. He will find also that a single text, even if it is geared to the average or slowest students in the class, will not provide adequately for the range of abilities and interests in every class. Most texts, because they cram too many topics into one cover, are not particularly interesting, and the teacher will soon find other sources which are much more stimulating. Consequently, he will use multiple texts or texts plus other materials. Following are some of the ways teachers have made use of textbooks, not as the sole basic book, but as one of the many books used in the classroom.

1. Texts on various levels were provided, and students worked individually at their own rate. This method is particularly successful with mathematics and can be

combined with the use of regular series of texts, work books, and programmed books.

2. Texts are frequently used as reference material for particular topics or units.

3. Certain texts with particularly good maps and charts can become a basis for discussion or written assignments in class.

4. Texts are used to teach particular reading skills—both reading texts and literature and social studies texts.

5. Questions and activities from certain textbooks may be used for homework assignments or class exercises.

Other Reading Material

Some teachers of disadvantaged children have been ingenious in finding material which can replace or supplement textbooks. Excellent trade books of fiction and biography written on all reading levels are now available, but many of these are too expensive for schools to purchase more than a few copies for each room. However these fine books are beginning to be printed in paperback. (Scholastic Book Services perhaps has the largest collection of material on all levels—fiction, biography, essays, text-type books, workbooks, and magazines.) There is also a trend now toward "packet material." These packages, in addition to booklets and pictures, usually provide a detailed lesson plan which some teachers will welcome, but most teachers like to make up their own plans and packets for classes or individuals. The same can be said for the individualized boxed material which has certain advantages but can become as much of a crutch as the old textbook approach if used exclusively. A creative teacher is always searching and collecting. Free materials from commercial enterprises and government agencies abound. Frequently an organization will supply whole class sets of material. This material may be used for total class or individual assignments. It may be used as it is, summarized, or "written down." It can be shown on the overhead projector. The problem the teacher usually has is how to use different kinds of material during the same class period and thereby provide for various ability levels. Following is a brief lesson plan showing how a teacher of a seventh-grade class (reading range 3.6 to 6.2) used three different pieces of reading matter.

Aim: To develop an understanding of why there is great poverty in Eastern Kentucky.

1. Using relief map, locate Kentucky. How would we get to Kentucky? In what direction would we be traveling?
2. Divide class into three groups according to reading level. Appoint group captain for each group. Give each group a different material, and explain that they are to read the assigned pages, and try to find the reason for the poverty stricken situation in Kentucky.
    A. Group   I—Arrow Book of States (Scholastic Book Services)
    B. Group II—How and Why Book (Grosset and Dunlap)
    C. Group III—Selection from *The Other America* by Michael Harrington[5]

Give each group a ditto sheet with questions.
    a. What product has been responsible for the poverty?
    b. Why don't the people move?
3. After students have read for about 15 minutes hold a class discussion.
    A. Have you discovered from your reading, the cause of the poverty in Kentucky? Why isn't there as much need for coal now? How many of you have a coal furnace? What has replaced coal? Where else has coal been replaced by some other product?
    B. If we lived in Kentucky, what business might we be in?
    C. How did Kentucky get its name? What does it mean? Why do you think that this is an appropriate name?
    D. How do many people in Kentucky manage to get

[5] A page from this book was simplified and mimeographed. It told of the current situation in Kentucky and contained more factual information than the other books.

along, if they don't work? How do you think these
people feel, being dependent on others?

E. Approximately how much does the average family
in Appalachia have to spend per week? What do
you think they manage to buy with this money?
Why don't people leave?

4. Hold up placards listing the products of Kentucky. Which
products would mean the development of large industrial
plants? Develop the point that this is largely an agricul-
tural and mining economy, with few other occupational
possibilities available at the present time. Let students try
to figure out how the people in Kentucky can be helped and
what other way of living might be developed.

ADDITIONAL TEACHING AIDS

Games are coming into vogue again especially in social
studies. The commercial games need to be judged like any
other material according to their appropriateness to the
class's ability and the goal of the particular unit or lesson.
Below-average students seem to like simple matching games.
These activities can help pupils learn to discriminate and
categorize. The more difficult games, which require a
higher degree of reasoning, need to be used carefully so that
students do not become discouraged. Teachers frequently
make up their own games, and these students, who are like
elementary school children, enjoy competing for prizes. As
long as the tasks are achievable, it would seem that competition does little harm except to an overanxious child who will
need to have an extra dose of encouragement.

The visual aids get better every day, and good films or
slides will often explain a concept or a fact better than the
written word. The overhead projector, because the teacher
can face the class, has many uses, and transparencies with
overlays are excellent for displaying maps, science experi-
ments, charts, graphs, and cartoons.

Disadvantaged students also like to make posters, puppets,
dioramas, murals, and other types of projects. The junior
high school teacher has seldom been trained in these skills

and frequently has a difficult time helping the students. In most schools the art or shop teacher will cooperate and let the student come in the shop for projects related to his other subjects. The teacher cannot expect work of high quality except from a talented few, but he should realize the tremendous satisfaction a child gets from displaying his wares and should encourage him in any creative efforts he is willing to pursue.

As mentioned previously, the tape recorder has multiple uses. Every room should have recorders and a set of earphones. Another new visual aid is the 8-millimeter single-concept loop film. This tiny portable machine may be viewed by individuals or small groups. The few schools which are equipped with these machines report enthusiastically.

These new machines and materials are not miraculous. Without the pupils' confident trust in the teacher and the teacher's skill and joy in helping the pupils learn, little can be accomplished. "Hard" and "soft ware" can only be *handmaidens.*

CONCLUSION

In these last two chapters you will note that the class activities cited were often more than a means to an end. In other words, the process (or activity) itself was the end as well as the means. Although the understanding or memorization of a particular bit of content might be one of the goals, a habit of concentration was also being established, an act of analyzing was being performed, or a desire for discovery developed. The method the teacher uses to direct or guide an activity is of prime importance. He avoids procedures which call for meaningless drill, unnecessary repetition, and diffuse and wasteful discussion. Instead he provides diverse, rich, and concrete experiences. He assists the child in the development of a logical progression of ideas, but he also makes room for activities which call forth imagination and creativity. Total class discussion, small-group discussion, individual

reading and writing, group projects, dramatization, role playing, and games all can be used by the insightful and flexible
teacher while he learns about the students' needs and desires. You will enjoy varying your approaches to teaching,
and your students will appreciate the variety.

QUESTIONS FOR DISCUSSION

Committee Reports

In a ninth-grade class (reading range 6 to 11) a teacher
tells how he launched a unit on Latin America by assigning
individual reports.

I listed all the countries on the board, and I asked the students
to take notes. I told them I expected their reports to contain information about the geography, the history, the government, the
economy, and the social aspects of the particular country they
were assigned. I asked them to include under geography:
location, population, climate, natural environment, natural resources. In history there should be information about settle-
ment of the country, colonial period, the independence, participation in Latin American affairs, participation in world affairs,
important people and important dates. Under government I
wanted to include information about type of colonial government, the government after independence, and success of both
of these types of government and also a description and analysis of present government that exists in the country. Under
economy I wanted to include information about colonial economy, economy after independence and the present economy,
the factor that was slowing down the economy or economic development, importance of mechanization to their economy, the
importance of finding investments or aid to the country, present
plans for development of the economy, and present position and
progress along those plans in the economy. Then, finally, on
social aspects I wanted to include discussion of the cultural her-
itage, customs, language, religion, education, recreation and
social class problems if there were any. These were the basic
factors I wanted each of the students to get on each of his
particular countries. I gave them each a country to work on in
South America. For some of the countries I put two students

on the topic to work individually, or if they decided to split the topic, they could present the material in the way they split the topic.   The major problem which I suggested to the class and which I will give them permission to change or alter was "How are Latin Americans solving their problems?"

After the individual reports were given, which the teacher felt were not too successful because many were just copied out of books verbatim or were very sparse and did not contain the most significant facts, the teacher decided to have committee reports.   He now wanted to have the children consider Latin America as a whole and assigned committees on geography, culture, and economy.   Below is his account of one of the committee reports.

One particular lesson which did not go over very well was a lesson with class 9–24 on Monday.   It was the lesson that the geography committee of our unit on Latin America presented. One of the children did not have a topic because he was out of class—he had not worked with his other class members to get this organized.   Another child gave a very poor report, not really knowing anything about his subject.   He was the committee chairman.   Another child didn't have a report ready.   Another boy had a committee problem that was completely confusing and poorly worded and impossible to answer.   One boy on the committee had a very good report and was able to tell just what he knew and was very familiar with his subject. Therefore, the lesson had to be reorganized and restated by me and by some of the class members in our evaluation and questions which were put to the committeemen.   All in all, the lesson was poorly organized for the following reasons: first of all, the children had not gotten the understanding of what they were supposed to present, except for one or two of them; those that did understand what they were to present were unable to get the information and present it with some semblance of knowledge or understanding of the problems and the materials that they had to prepare for us.
There is another thing that is also a weakness.   These children were not familiar with the method of stating a problem and then understanding what the problem meant and then answering it. Perhaps they had not had enough time with me to work on this, to iron out the difficulties.   So, therefore, I can blame myself for

a good part of their failure to produce results. But inasmuch as one child was able to get through with the material in the committee, and only one, I suggest that he was bright enough to understand what he was doing and the others were not bright enough to understand it and did need more cooperation and help which I was unable to give them. The problem with this committee is that I had covered geography and some of the problems that they were considering in class, and they should have been familiar with the material. In fact, the class appeared to be a little bit more aware of what was going on than the committee people who were supposed to have prepared the subject. All in all, it was rather unsuccessful to attempt to present geographic factors or problems of Latin America to the class, but it was supplemented by questions and points of information which covered the subject by discussion instead of presentation by a committee. Concerning the class's reaction, they were rather bored with the whole thing and reasonably so.

1. What was wrong with these individual assignments?
2. How much and what type of information about the countries of Latin America would you feel essential for an average ninth-grade class?
3. How could you make the assignment meaningful and more interesting?
4. To what extent could you expect children to carry on research organized around these topics? What are some of the ways of teaching research skills?
5. In addition to a series of individual reports, what are other ways of sharing information?
6. When the teacher organized the class into three groups for committee reports, he was also disappointed in the results. Why is group work so often unsuccessful?
7. How should the teacher have prepared his class for group work? Was the teacher probably right in saying that he had not helped them enough in stating the problem? What else would he need to do to assure some success? Why did he not know they were unprepared?
8. When should group work be used? What attitudes and skills is it designed to teach? Why does it often fail to do so?

SUGGESTED READING

Amidon, Edmund, and Elizabeth Hunter:
Improving Teaching: The Analysis of Classroom Verbal Interaction,
Holt, Rinehart and Winston, Inc., New York, 1966.
Bruner, Jerome S.:
The Process of Education,
Harvard University Press, Cambridge, Mass., 1961.
Niblett, W. R. (ed.):
How and Why Do We Learn?
Faber & Faber, Ltd., London, 1965.
Sanders, Norris M.:
Classroom Questions: What Kinds?
Harper & Row, Publishers, Incorporated, New York, 1966.
Strom, Robert D.:
Teaching in the Slum School,
Charles E. Merrill Books, Inc., Columbus, Ohio, 1965, chap. 5.
Taba, Hilda, and Deborah Elkins:
Teaching Strategies for the Culturally Disadvantaged,
Rand McNally & Company, Chicago, 1966, chaps. 4, 13.

Epilogue
IN THREE YEARS' TIME

It has often been said that because personality, habits, and attitudes are formed in early childhood, little change can be made in junior high school students. In the past, in many junior high slum schools, academic progress slowed down even more than in elementary school, and the reading level of the pupils seldom advanced more than one year between the sixth and tenth grades. We know now, however, that with the attention being given to compensatory education—smaller classes, appropriate material, and skillful teaching—many children can make more progress than was formerly thought possible.

The account that follows is taken from the Bridge Project records.   As you read it, note carefully the elementary record and the junior high teachers' comments about this particular student in the seventh grade and again in the ninth.

CASE STUDY REPORT

NAME: *Babbett Brewer*

RECORD OF ELEMENTARY SCHOOL:

BORN: 9/7/48   Class 7–3   CA 13–4
SIBLINGS: Older—1 brother
                  Younger—1 brother
         Lives in Project apartment
         Both parents work
SCHOOL EXPERIENCE: Entered 9/54
         Brown Elementary School—Grades 1 through 6
                                   (Held over in Grade 4) 1958

ADDITIONAL INFORMATION:

5/57   Mother up to see about Babbett's work after being repeatedly sent for.   Mother seems unwilling to cooperate.   When told that the child needs help in reading she responded that it wouldn't be possible.

6/57   Child tried to strangle self and began shouting and crying and threatening other children.

6/58   Very lazy.   Does little or no work.   Reported for writing on walls of girls' room.   Has very few friends.   Claims she is mistreated at home; that no one is interested in her.

4/60   Mr. A. and principal discussed possibility of again "holding back" Babbett for another year.

COUNSELOR INTERVIEW:

Expressed doubts about mother's feelings for her. ... Doubts that people like her if they do not show concrete evidence of it. Shows enthusiasm about school and her teachers. ...

SPECIAL ABILITY: Vocal music
INTERESTS: Dance, TV
GOALS: Nurse

TEST DATA:

5/55	Pintner Cunningham	IQ 116
3/57	Otis Alpha	IQ 100
10/60	Otis Beta	IQ 70

JUNIOR HIGH SCHOOL TESTING RECORD:

11/61	WISC*		IQ 89
Metropolitan Reading		Grade 7	3.0
		Grade 8	4.9
		Grade 9	6.1

JUNIOR HIGH SCHOOL TEACHERS' REPORTS

SEVENTH GRADE: REPORT BY TEACHER A
(English, Female)

Physical Characteristics: Babbett is a very tall girl and extremely heavy. I remember very well the time the class called her the elephant. She is not attractive mainly because of her weight. It's very difficult for her to dress well, but she has been looking a great deal better than she had before. She is naturally hampered by her weight in moving around.

Behavior: In English Babbett does very little work and absolutely no homework. She doesn't do what is expected of her, and she seems to feel that she deserves special treat-

* Wechsler Intelligence Scale for Children.

ment, and I have no possible clue as to why. Yet, during Open School Week, she came to me and asked if I needed help and she did do a lot of work for me. She went down and got me coffee and all this kind of thing, so that I don't feel it's a definite problem between Babbett and me, but something about the assignments and the routines of English that she doesn't like.

Babbett seems to need a close friend with whom she can confide. She needs a great deal of approval and I think she feels very inadequate in the field of language.

I think that Babbett has a definite problem because of her weight. The other students make fun of her. They call her Mrs. J. all the time. They make Jimmy's life miserable by associating him with her. They do this just to tease Jimmy and Babbett is very hurt by it. She has a very poor self-image because of her size and her inability to cope with the work. She is not popular and has very little self-confidence.

Academic Work: Babbett does not speak well, read well or write well. Her memory is fair. I have no idea what her interests are. I think her intellectual potential is dull normal. She displays little effort or persistence, and accomplishes practically nothing. However she has begun to do a little bit of work. She never used to take a spelling test. Now she is at least studying and taking a spelling test and doing fairly well in that. It's a little step in the right direction. Also I think that I found out various things of late. She sits right across from Walter who speaks to me fairly often, and he comes back and tells me everything she says, and she talks mainly about my size. I think she resents the fact that I'm thin and she's not, and she keeps coming and asking me if I needed help.

Best Classroom Approach: Since I don't have any, this leads directly into the question: What is the best way for me to handle Babbett?

NINTH GRADE

Physical Characteristics: Babbett is a tall, buxom girl who really should lose some weight. She is very conscious of her weight, although not so much as formerly. She has dark brown skin, a nice clear complexion, and short, somewhat unmanageable hair. Babbett has a large frame, and can be classified as a big, pleasant-looking girl.

Behavior: In the beginning Babbett was sullen and resentful, and she cut classes frequently. She refused to do any of the classwork or homework. She refused to take any of the tests. Consequently she received failing grades on her report in my class and the pattern worsened. The situation was so bad that Babbett would do anything to get out of coming to English class, inventing every kind of job to get permission to stay out.

This September Babbett came back a changed girl. She now attacks her work with a vigor unequalled by anyone in the lower classes. She does all her homework. She spends her class time shushing all those in the class who talk and disturb her. She is a new girl.

One day after about three weeks of this term had gone by, Babbett came to see me privately. She was bursting with smiles and happiness when she said "Oh Miss A, I love English this year. I never liked it before, but this year I really like it." Since that time she has received good grades.

Academic Work: For the first two years Babbett said she had always hated English. Her reasons for hating the subject were simple. She was very poor at it, and couldn't accept the failure especially since she was beginning to do well in all her other subjects.

Babbett will never be a good English student but now she is willing to try her very best, knowing that it will not be perfect. She seems much more accepting of herself, both her appearance and her abilities.

Babbett is one of our sample who has gone up phenomenally in reading. She is now on about a high sixth grade level. She is still a very poor speller and writer, but is getting better rapidly, as her success in class indicates.

Additional Information: The greatest thing has happened in Babbett's life; she has found something she loves to do. She is a volunteer worker at the hospital. She takes her job very seriously. She started there during the summer, and stayed during the year on Saturdays because she liked it so much.   She wishes to do nursing as a career.

Babbett is very proud of her work at the hospital, as she should be.   The work has given her a great boost in self-confidence, which she desperately needed.   It has given her a new outlook on life.   It has given her something to talk about to others her age.   It has also provided her with work that she really could do well.   She has had the feeling of having other people depend on her, and she has felt the rewards of giving.   It has made her a much stronger person.

Babbett's father is a mason who participates in his organization.   He goes to frequent meetings—has received honor in his organization.   Babbett is very proud of him.   He looks very young in his pictures.

Reactions to Last Report: At the time of the first report I only guessed, now I know, that Babbett hated English work. This year all that has changed as I have said before.   At the time of the last report Babbett was constantly being teased about her work and she couldn't take it.   Now she is rarely teased, and when she is, it hardly bothers her.   Babbett now has gained self-confidence.   She responds well to all classroom routines.   Babbett was an exceptionally poor student; now she is one of the two best students in her class.   Babbett's and my relationship has improved in geometric progression.   She is now one of my favorite people, whereas she was one of my poorest students and not one of my favorites by any means.

SEVENTH GRADE: REPORT BY TEACHER B
(Social Studies, Male)

Physical Characteristics: Babbett is a tall girl and quite heavy.   At the beginning of the term she seemed to be sloppy and unconcerned about her appearance.   Lately she has been dressing more neatly and seems genuinely concerned about her appearance.   She moves slowly because of her weight.   She often complains about pains in her legs and told me that she has difficulty walking up the stairs.

Behavior: I get along quite well with Babbett.   The first few days of the term she seemed quite unhappy about talking to me but since then she has become almost a new person. She is anxious to do anything for me. She is quite happy when I help her with her work. She works much better when the personal approach is used. She seems quite interested in and fond of her teachers as people and I feel that she feels very much at home in school. I like Babbett very much. She makes me feel as if I am accomplishing something, and I am always very glad to take as much extra time as necessary to help her. She is always grateful when she receives help. Babbett seems especially fond of Miss C. She is always talking to me about the things that Miss C. does. She tries to imitate her in every way possible. I've noticed that she's even picked up some of the idioms that Miss C. uses.

At the beginning of the term Babbett didn't get along very well with most of the pupils in her class. They called her "elephant" and made fun of her. Often she would cry as a result of this. After a while she became friendly with a few of the girls. They like working with her. She works very well in pairs or with groups of her classmates. She has very little to do with the boys apart from occasional name calling. Often the boys tend to anger Babbett. I remember her really beating up one of the boys when he called her some sort of name.

Babbett is quite a sensitive, delicate youngster. She notices many things that you would expect only an adult to notice. She cries at the slightest provocation and angers very easily however.

Babbett is willing to give affection but she also expects a great deal in return. She wants to feel that she is liked and appreciated. She seems to need recognition from her teachers very badly.

Babbett wants to be a nurse. I think that this is an unrealistic aim, but she should be encouraged to go into a related field. She works wonderfully well with people. She has tremendous compassion for people, and becomes disturbed when other people are sad. This is a trait often lacking in many of our students.

Babbett follows routines well. She follows instructions although she often has difficulty following them.

Babbett definitely lacks self-confidence. I think that she feels set apart and strange in the class and therefore she makes a special attempt to get close to the teachers.

Academic Work: At the beginning of the term when an assignment was given Babbett used to sit down and start crying. She seemed unable to cope with the work. After a few weeks as she started to get involved in the reading club she started to do the work. At the present time she works better than any of the other pupils in the class. When an assignment is given she jumps into it right away. She keeps doing it until it gets done, or until she is unable to continue further because of lack of knowledge. She genuinely loved *Squanto.* Often she comes into the room and asks if she can borrow the book so that she could reread one of the chapters. I don't believe that Babbett has too much ability, but she seems to be using all that she has.

After five months of school, Babbett seems happier, healthier and more well adjusted than at the beginning of the term.

NINTH GRADE

Physical Characteristics: Babbett is quite a tall girl, and she remains quite overweight. She has embarked upon a number of diets, but like all of us, the battle of the bulge remains one of her major concerns. She is concerned with her appearance. She is neat and well dressed, and one of the most personable youngsters we have in our sample. Babbett seems to have difficulty getting around as quickly as she would like to. She tires easily, and seems to contract colds easily.

Behavior: Babbett is one of the children with whom we have had the most success over the three years. When she came to us, she was a child that was extremely unhappy. She cried at the slightest provocation, she refused to participate in classroom activities, and seemed to be unhappy with everything. After a couple of months she started adjusting to her surroundings, and there has been a slow gradual change until today we find her more outgoing, pleasant, happy with school, happier to be here than home, and generally content with herself, and what she has done.

Babbett is a member of the Service Squad in the school. She participates in extra curricular activities. She knows most of the other teachers in the school, from various contacts she has made, and is generally content with herself, and what she has done.

Babbett is one of my favorite youngsters. She is one of our few stalwarts on a day when everything else seems to go wrong. She is anxious to work. She will help to the utmost of her ability. She often assumes the role of class housekeeper, in taking care of certain things which must be done.

Babbett has been switched from one class to another, and we find that she is best in the slowest class.[1] Even this year she was put in my official class, and we found that she was unable to do the work, and felt quite unhappy about it, so she was put back in 9–3 and seems to be doing fine.

Babbett has definitely noticed the boys, but they don't seem to have noticed her. She is teased, and bothered, and is not above losing her temper, and whacking them when they deserve it.

Babbett has a number of friends among the girls. She seems to be good friends with Geraldine and a few others. Socially I think that she's more advanced than those in 9–3, but academically she fits in very well there.

It is really a pleasure to have Babbett in the classroom, you can always count on her to be attentive, and aware of what is going on.

Academic Work: Babbett has made tremendous progress in her reading. Apart from intermittant periods when she becomes negligent, she is constantly reading something. I try to give her as many books about nursing as possible, as she reads them quickly and with tremendous interest. Her word attack skills have improved. She enjoys reading in front of the class. The minute we do oral reading her hand

---

[1] The three Bridge teachers were permitted to switch children from one group to another if they felt the children would do better with another group.

shoots up. She reads and then when everyone is finished, she wants to read again. She seems to have an insatiable desire to perform as much as possible. I'm usually happy to let her do so, as she needs it. Needless to say there is no comparison between the way that she reads now and the way she did when she came to us, just as there is no comparison in her composure, way of working, or her attitude.

In Social Studies, Babbett does what is expected of her, but doesn't excell the way she does in reading. I noticed that when we studied history she complained that she wasn't interested. This year, since the subject matter is related to the world today, she participates with somewhat greater vigor. When there is an assignment to read, she does it well, but when we have a discussion, her involvement ranges from minimal to mediocre.

SEVENTH GRADE: REPORT BY TEACHER C
(Math, Science, and Homeroom, Female)

Physical Characteristics: Babbett is a very large child. She is obviously overweight and doesn't try to do anything about losing weight. Babbett is a very tall girl, and looks well developed for her age. Nevertheless, she does not wear provocative clothing. She has a rather slow moving gait, and an average to low energy level.

Behavior: I have never had any kind of behavior problem with Babbett since the beginning of the term. She tries very hard to please. At first, I noticed that Babbett was constantly depressed. In September and October, she cried a lot. She used to say, "Today is one of my sad days." She spoke to me once and told me that her aunt told her that any one who was so depressed must be crazy. She asked me what I thought. . . . She also complained of having menstrual difficulties which she said bothered her. She goes to the doctor very often about a back complaint. She also complained of headaches.

Now, I can honestly say that Babbett has improved. She no longer gets "depressed," and she loves school. She has been working very hard and has related well to her teachers. She seems to gain a great deal of satisfaction from her work and is not as troubled about her home problems as she was before.   (I got the impression that Babbett is not sure of her mother's love and was constantly testing her teachers when she first started school.)   She has also been interested in pursuing her desires to become a nurse.

Academic Work: Babbett *is* working, but I'm afraid that she has more ability than her tests results show.   Babbett has picked up tremendously in her reading, and has done much better in her math.   She still has a long way to go, but with constant encouragement, I think Babbett will make it.   I am hopeful that Babbett will make it to high school and perhaps train to become a nurse's aid.

Her written work is poor, but I have seen an improvement.

Additional Information: From Babbett I can gather that her home life could be happier.   I know that there is a mother and a father.   I was told by her mother that she has a married son who has children.   Babbett often takes care of her nieces and nephews.   She does work after school caring for a year old child.   She enjoys her work and often talks about it.   She has a cousin in the 8th year.   They were very close and enjoy being together.

I am not worried about Babbett; she has really shown improvement in all respects.   I think with constant encouragement she will continue to do well.   I believe she is one of our most promising students.

NINTH GRADE

Physical Characteristics: Babbett is about 5′ 8″ and overweight.   She is presently under the care of the Q.G. Weight Clinic—and she has lost about 8 lbs.   She is always neat and clean, but she has a limited wardrobe.   She has a good attendance record and no latenesses.   She very rarely complains of any aches or pains these days as she did in her first year.

Behavior: Babbett is always well behaved.   She has excellent manners.   She will always listen in class unless something is really troubling her. She will often yell at the others when they don't listen, and they do listen to Babbett. She is well liked—takes a lot of kidding from the boys about her weight—but she laughs and jokes with them. They really like her now. She will often intercede in a fight and try to settle arguments. She really hates fighting or violence of any kind.

The day President Kennedy was assassinated she cried bitterly—she said, "When will people learn to live with one another peacefully?"

Academic Work: Babbett has improved in every area. First we thought she ought to be in the 2 class—then we found she worked better in the 3—the pace was slower. Her reading has made a miraculous jump—3rd to 6.0 and we hope at least to 7.0 so she can receive a diploma. She does well in Math—likes Science—and is voraciously interested in everything about nursing.

Babbett wants to be a nurse more than she wants anything in the world. She has done volunteer work at the Hospital for the summer and she goes every available holiday and Saturday. She has gone by herself and on her own through the membership in the Future Nurses Club. She has become very active and is happy with her work. She was the grade representative in the assembly and spoke to all the assemblies about the Red Cross Drive. We were all so proud of her.

She continues her class work—her volunteer work and her extra curricular duties. She is interested in the welfare of the students and the school. She is well liked, and very much appreciated. Thank God for our Babbett.

Additional Information: I have often wondered what I would write when it came to telling about Babbett. For all of the dismal days—the frustrating lessons—the battles with the administration and just "days"—Babbett has made all of the work we have done so far the most worthwhile work in the world. We have seen a little chubby retiring, frightened child (7th year) become a lovely confident young lady.

Babbett, you recall, was a very sensitive frightened girl. She had no confidence in herself, and cried about everything. We all decided that Babbett had what it takes, and slowly we tried to help her build confidence in herself. Babbett needed so much love and attention we tried to give it to her.

QUESTIONS FOR DISCUSSION

1. What is your overall reaction to the teachers' reports on Babbett?
2. Do you believe that they tried to get at the heart of Babbett's problems?
3. What were the "potentials" for change in Babbett's personality—as described by the teachers?
4. Do you believe the "outside job" was the most significant factor in Babbett's change of attitude toward schoolwork?
5. What kind of future do you predict for Babbett?

A child in the Bridge Project, when asked to write what she liked best about the three years, wrote, "Well, best I liked the teachers and the way they helped us learn new things. We just liked them period. Truly too."
We hope your students will say the same about you.

H. S.

BIBLIOGRAPHY

Amidon, Edmund, and Elizabeth Hunter:
Improving Teaching, The Analysis of Classroom Verbal Interaction,
Holt, Rinehart and Winston, Inc., New York, 1966.

Ausubel, David P.:
The Psychology of Meaningful Verbal Learning,
Grune & Stratton, Inc., New York, 1963.

————:
"A Teaching Strategy for Culturally Deprived Pupils: Cognitive and Motivational Considerations,"
The School Review, vol. 71, pp. 458–463, Winter, 1963.

Bard, Harry:
Home-work: A Guide for Secondary School Teachers,
Holt, Rinehart and Winston, Inc., New York, 1958.

Bloom, Benjamin, Allison Davis, and Robert Hess:
Compensatory Education for Cultural Deprivation,
Holt, Rinehart and Winston, Inc., New York, 1965.

Bruner, Jerome S.:
Toward a Theory of Instruction,
Harvard University Press, Cambridge, Mass., 1960.

Burton, William H.:
The Guidance of Learning Activities,
Appleton-Century-Crofts, Inc., New York, 1962.

Conant, James:
Slums and Suburbs,
McGraw-Hill Book Company, New York, 1961.

Crow, Lester D., Walter I. Murray, and Hugh H. Smythe:
Educating the Culturally Disadvantaged Child,
David McKay Company, Inc., New York, 1966.

Downing, Gertrude, Robert W. Edgar, Albert J. Harris, Leonard Kornberg, and Helen F. Storen:
The Preparation of Teachers for Schools in Culturally Deprived Neighborhoods
(The Bridge Project: Cooperative Research Project no. 935, U.S. Office of Education),
Queens College of The City University of New York, Flushing, N.Y., 1965.

Edgar, Robert, and Carl Auria:
The Impact of Learning and Retention of
Specially Developed History Materials for Culturally

Deprived Children: An Exploratory Study
(Cooperative Research Small Contract Project S265,
U.S. Office of Education),
The Research Foundation of The City University of New York,
New York, 1966.
The Educationally Retarded and Disadvantaged,
The Sixty-sixth Yearbook of the National Society for the
Study of Education, edited by Paul A. Witty,
The University of Chicago Press, Chicago, 1967.
Frost, Joe L., and Glenn R. Hawkes:
The Disadvantaged Child: Issues and Innovations,
Houghton Mifflin Company, Boston, 1966.
Gordon, Edmund W., and Doxey A. Wilkerson:
*Compensatory Education for the Disadvantaged: Programs
and Practices: Pre-school through College,*
College Entrance Examination Board, New York, 1967.
Holbrook, David:
English for the Rejected,
Cambridge University Press, London, 1964.
Jewett, Arno, Joseph Mersand, and Doris Gunderson (eds.):
*Improving English Skills of Culturally Different Youth in
Large Cities,*
U.S. Office of Education, Washington, 1964.
Johnson, Orville G.:
Education for the Slow Learners,
Prentice-Hall, Inc., Englewood Cliffs, N.J., 1963.
Levine, Daniel:
"Differentiating Instruction for Disadvantaged Students,"
Educational Forum, vol. 30, no. 2, pp. 144–145, January, 1966.
McGeogh, Dorothy, C. R. Bloomgarden, Ellen O. Furedi, Lynne
W. Randolph, and Eugene D. Ruth, Jr.:
Learning to Teach in Urban Schools,
Teachers College Press, Columbia University, New York, 1965.
Muus, Rolf:
First Aid for Classroom Discipline Problems,
Holt, Rinehart and Winston, Inc., New York, 1962.
Niblitt, W. R. (ed.):
How and Why Do We Learn?,
Faber and Faber, Ltd., London, 1965.
Passow, A. Harry (ed.):
Education in Depressed Areas,

Teachers College Press, Columbia University, New York, 1963.
————, Miriam Goldberg, and Abraham J. Tannenbaum (eds.):
Education of the Disadvantaged: A Book of Readings,
Holt, Rinehart and Winston, Inc.,
New York, 1967.
Reisman, Frank:
The Culturally Deprived Child,
Harper and Row, Publishers, Incorporated, New York, 1962.
Sanders, Norris M.:
Classroom Questions: What Kinds?,
Harper and Row, Publishers, Incorporated, New York, 1966.
Sears, Pauline, and Ernest Hilgard:
"The Teacher's Role in the Motivation of the Learner,"
Theories of Learning and Instruction,
The Sixty-third Yearbook of the National Society
for the Study of Education,
The University of Chicago Press, 1965, part I, chap. 8.
Storen, Helen F., and Robert Edgar:
Learning To Teach in Difficult Schools
(Bridge Project Publication no. 4),
Queens College of The City University of New York,
Flushing, N.Y., 1963.

————:

The First Semester: Beginning Teachers in Urban Schools,
Project TRUE, Hunter College of The City University of
New York, 1965.

————:

"Making up the Deficit,"
The Clearing House, vol. 39, no. 8, pp. 495–499, April, 1965.
Strom, Robert D.:
Teaching in the Slum School,
Charles E. Merrill Books, Inc., Columbus, Ohio, 1965.
———— (ed.):
The Inner-city Classroom: Teacher Behaviors,
Charles E. Merrill Books, Inc., Columbus, Ohio, 1966.
Taba, Hilda, and Deborah Elkins:
Teaching Strategies for the Culturally Disadvantaged,
Rand McNally & Company, Chicago, 1966.
————, Samuel Levine, and Elzay Freeman:
Thinking in Elementary School Children
(Cooperative Research Project no. 1574,

U.S. Office of Education),
San Francisco State College, San Francisco, California, 1965.
Tansley, A. E., and R. Gulliford:
The Education of Slow Learning Children,
Routledge & Kegan Paul, Ltd., London, 1961.

INDEX